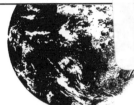

A spirit child has far to go . . .

BEN OKRI
THE
FAMISHED ROAD

Ben Okri will be reading from *The Famished Road*
at the Cottesloe Auditorium, Royal National Theatre,
South Bank, London SE1 on Tuesday 9 April at 6pm.
Tickets £2.00 from the Box Office Tel: 071 928 2252

Published by Jonathan Cape   21 March   £13.99

ISBN 0 224 02712 3

THE UNBEARABLE PEACE

35

Editor: Bill Buford
Deputy Editor: Tim Adams
Managing Editor: Ursula Doyle
Contributing Editor: Lucretia Stewart

Managing Director: Derek Johns
Financial Manager: Geoffrey Gordon
Publishing Assistant: Sally Lewis
Production Assistant: Stephen Taylor

Picture Editor: Alice Rose George
Picture Research: Sally Lewis
Design: Chris Hyde
Executive Editor: Pete de Bolla
US Associate Publisher: Anne Kinard, Granta, 250 West 57th Street, Suite 1316, New York, NY 10107.

Editorial and Subscription Correspondence: Granta, 2-3 Hanover Yard, Noel Road, Islington, London N1 8BE. Telephone: (071) 704 9776. Fax: (071) 704 0474. Subscriptions: (071) 837 7765.
A one-year subscription (four issues) is £19.95 in Britain, £25.95 for the rest of Europe, and £31.95 for the rest of the world.
All manuscripts are welcome but must be accompanied by a stamped, self-addressed envelope or they cannot be returned.

Cover by Alex Kayser.

Granta 35, Spring 1991

ISBN 014-01-5204-0

The roguish wit's portrait of bohemian London plus six of his most brilliant wartime stories

'Remarkable artistry . . . a beautifully executed period piece' NEW STATESMAN

'Mr Hamilton is one of the best English novelists' JOHN BETJEMAN

'Unfaltering in design and pace . . . thoroughly inspiring' MAIL ON SUNDAY

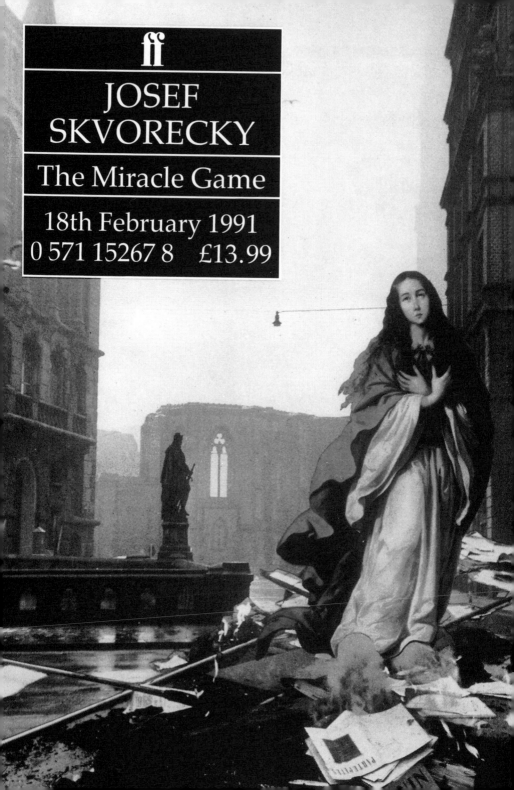

ff

JOSEF SKVORECKY

The Miracle Game

18th February 1991
0 571 15267 8   £13.99

CONTENTS

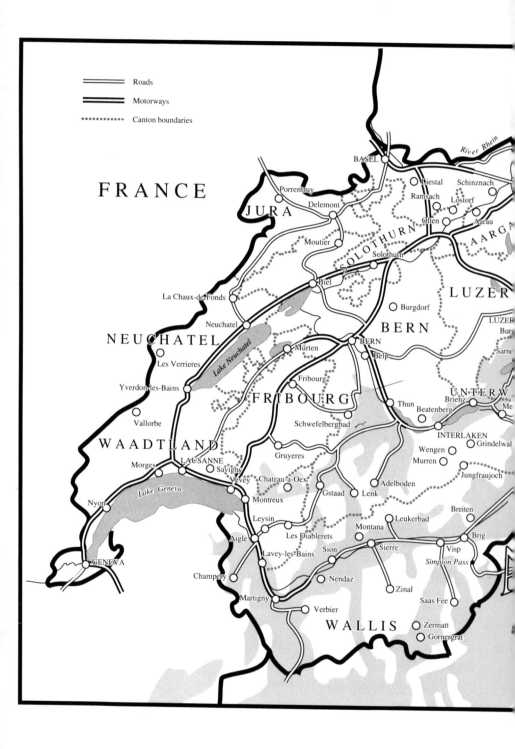

THE ROYAL COURT THEATRE'S PRODUCTION OF

TOP GIRLS

BY CARYL CHURCHILL

Max Stafford-Clark directs the first major revival since its first performance at the Royal Court in 1982 when it received enormous critical acclaim both in London and New York. Opening at the Arts Centre University of Warwick the production will then tour to Bath, Blackpool, Cambridge and London.

In an original and unexpected first scene five women from history celebrate their extraordinary achievements with Marlene, a top executive.

The story then focuses on what Marlene has given up for her career and the values she has had to embrace. In the play's final scene the ambitious Marlene argues it out with Joyce, the sister who stayed behind.

'a dramatist who must surely be rated among the half dozen best now writing'
BENEDICT NIGHTINGALE, NEW STATESMAN

WITH
DEBORAH FINDLAY · BETH GODDARD · CECILY HOBBS · SARAH LAM · LESLEY MANVILLE
· ANNA PATRICK · LESLEY SHARP ·

5 - 9 March · Arts Centre, University of Warwick (0203) 524524
12 - 16 · March Grand Theatre Blackpool (0253) 28372
18 - 23 March· Theatre Royal Bath (0225) 448844
2 - 6 April · Cambridge Arts Theatre (0223) 355246
from 10 April · Royal Court Theatre 071-730 1745 cc 071 836 2428

ROYAL
COURT
THEATRE

GRANTA

JOHN LE CARRÉ
THE UNBEARABLE PEACE

'I didn't die,' says Jeanmaire proudly. 'They wanted me to, but I wouldn't do them the favour.'

It is evening. We are alone in his tiny flat on the eastern outskirts of Bern. He is cooking cheese fondue for the two of us. On a shelf in the kitchen stand the steel eating bowls he used in prison. Why does he keep them?

'For memory,' he replies.

In the tiny corridor outside hang the dagger and sabre that are the insignia of a Swiss army officer's dress uniform. The drawing-room is decorated with a reproduction medieval halberd and his diploma of architecture dated 1934. A signed photograph from General Westmoreland, commemorating a goodwill visit to Bern, is inscribed 'General, Air Protection Troops', Jeanmaire's last appointment.

'Of course there were some of my colleagues who got nothing,' he says slyly, indicating that he was singled out for this distinction.

He has decided it is time for a drink. He drinks frugally these days, but still with the relish for which he is remembered.

'I permit myself a little water,' he announces. Prussian style, he stiffens his back, raises his elbow, whips the cap off the whisky bottle I have brought him and pours two precise shots. He adds his water; we raise our glasses, drink eye to eye, raise them again, then perch ourselves awkwardly at the table while he rolls the whisky round his mouth and declares it drinkable. Then he is off again, this time to the oven to stir the cheese and—as a trained and tried military instructor as well as judge—lecture me on how to do it on my own next time.

On the desk, and on the floor, and piled high against the wall, papers, files, press cuttings, mounds of them, mustered and flagged for his last campaign.

It is a journalistic conceit to pretend you are unmoved by people. But I am not a journalist and I am not superior to this encounter. Jean-Louis Jeanmaire moves me deeply and humorously and horribly.

Opposite: Jean-Louis Jeanmaire photographed in his apartment in the suburbs of Bern, 8 January 1991.

Jeanmaire is not cut out to be a mystery, least of all a spy. He is not cut out to be a Swiss, for his feelings are written all over his features, even when he is trying to hide them, and he would be the worst poker player in the world. He is broad-faced and, for a seemingly aggressive man, strangely vulnerable. He has the eyebrows of an angry clown. They lift and scowl and flit and marvel with every stray mood that passes over him. His body too is seldom reconciled. He seems to come at you and retreat at the same time. He is short and was once delicate, but striving has made a bull of him. His brief, passionate gestures are the more massive for being confined in a small room. Wherever you are with him in his life—whether in his childhood, or in the Army, or in his marriage, or in court, or in prison—you feel in him, and sometimes in yourself as well, the need for greater space, more air, more distance.

'I had no *access* to top secret information!' he whispers, with an emotional implosion that his body seems hardly able to contain. 'How could I have betrayed secrets I didn't know? All I ever did was give the Russians harmless bits of proof that Switzerland was a dangerous country to attack!' A wave of anger seizes him. '*C'était la dissuasion*,' he bellows. He is wagging his finger at me. His brows are clamped together above his nose. 'My aim was to deter those mad Bolsheviks at the Kremlin from mounting an assault against my country! I showed them how expensive it would be! What is *dissuasion* if the other side is not *dissuaded*? Denissenko understood that! We were working together against the Bolsheviks!'

His voice drops to make the point more gently: 'I was never a traitor. A fool maybe. A traitor, never!'

He has no time between moods. He has no time. He is pursuing justice every moment that is left to him. He can act and mime. He can camp and scorn and laugh. He has the energy of a man half his eighty years. One minute he is squared at you like a boxer; the next all you have to look at is his soldier's back as, toes and heels together, he bows devotionally to light the candles on the tiny kitchen table. He lights them every day in memory of his dead wife, he says: the

14

same wife whom he never once blamed for sleeping with his Nemesis, the Soviet military attaché and intelligence officer Colonel Vassily Denissenko, Deni for short, who was stationed in Bern in the early sixties and effortlessly recruited Jeanmaire as his source.

He waves out the match. He has the tiny fingers of a watchmaker. 'But Deni was an attractive man!' he protests, as his far-off, pale eyes brim again with love remembered, whether for his wife or for Deni or for both of them. 'If I'd been a woman I'd have slept with him myself!'

The statement does not embarrass him. For all that has been done to him, Jeanmaire is a lover still: of his friends, dead or alive, of his several women and of his erstwhile Russian contacts. The ease with which a man so deceived in his loyalties continues to give his trust is terrifying. It is impossible to listen to him for any time and not wish to take him into your protection. Deni was handsome! he is insisting. Deni was cultivated, charming, honourable, a gentleman! Deni was a hero of Stalingrad, he had medals for gallantry, he admired the Swiss Army! Deni was no Bolshevik: he was a horseman, a czarist, an officer of the old school!

Deni, he might add, was also the acknowledged Resident of the GRU, or Soviet Military Intelligence Service, poor cousin of the KGB. But Jeanmaire doesn't seem to care. The first time he even heard of the KGB, he insists, was when he was cataloguing books for the prison library. The GRU remains even more remote from him. He swears that throughout his entire military career, he never had the least training in these bodies.

And Deni was *faithful to the end*, he repeats, driving his little fist on to the table like a child who fears he is unheard: the end being twelve years in solitary confinement in a cell ten feet by six, after 130 days of intermittent civilian and military interrogation while under arrest, followed by a further six months' detention while awaiting trial and a closed military tribunal that lasted barely four days. Its findings are still secret.

'When they arrested me, Deni wrote a letter from Moscow to the *Soviet Literary Gazette*, describing me as the greatest anti-communist he had ever known. The letter was published in the Swiss press but never referred to at my trial. That was exceptional, such a letter. Deni cared very much about me.'

That is not exactly what Denissenko wrote about him, but never mind. He described Jeanmaire as a nationalist and patriot, which is probably how Denissenko regarded himself also.

And still the anguished eulogy flows on. Deni never pressed him, never tried to squeeze anything out of him he didn't want to give. Ergo—Deni was an honourable man! Not so honourable that Jeanmaire would let Deni pay for drinks or that he could accept an envelope of money from him or even that he could let Deni get a sight of Jeanmaire's signature on a letter, but honourable all the same: 'Deni was a man of heart, a brother officer in the best sense!'

Above all, Deni was *noble*. Jeanmaire awards this word like a medal. Jeanmaire has been pre-judged, reviled and incarcerated. He has come as near to being burned as a witch as modern society allows. But all he asks is that, before he dies, the world will give him back his own nobility. And I hope it will. And so would all of us. For who can disappoint a man of such infectious and vulnerable feeling?

To the suggestion that he might have been jealous of his wife's lover, Jeanmaire expresses only mystification.

'*Jealousy?*' he repeats, as the nimble eyebrows rush together in disapproval. '*Jealousy?* Jealousy is the vice of a limited man, but trust—'

We have struck his vanity again, his tragic, childish, prickly vanity: Jeanmaire is not a limited man, he would have me know! And his wife was a pure, good, beautiful woman and, like Deni, faithful to the end! Even though, in his wife's case, the end came sooner, for she died while he was still in prison. Deni's charm, whatever else it had going for it, did not come cheap.

From the pile of cuttings Jeanmaire extracts a muddy photograph of the great man, and I try hard to imagine his allure. Or was the allure actually all on Jeanmaire's side, and was Jeanmaire the one person who never knew it? Alas, Russian officers are seldom photogenic. All I see in Deni is a grey-suited, doughy-faced military bureaucrat of no expression, looking as if he would prefer not to have been photographed at all. And Jeanmaire, this un-Swiss Swiss, beaming as if he has just won the Derby.

L et me be a journalist for a moment. Jean-Louis Jeanmaire was born in 1910 in the small industrial town of Biel in the canton of Bern, where they do indeed make, among other things, the watches that remind me of his little hands. Biel is bilingual, German and French. So is Jeanmaire, though he regards French as his first language and speaks German with a grating, nasal pseudo-Prussian accent that to my ear is not at all Swiss, but then I was never in the Swiss Army. If there were such a thing as German Canadian, I am thinking as I listen to the rolled *r*s and saw-edged *a*s, that is what Jeanmaire would be speaking. His father was an arch-conservative of chilling rectitude. Like Jean-Louis after him, he was a chartered architect. But by passion he was a Colonel of Cavalry and Commandant of Mobilization for the town of Biel. In a country condemned to peace, the infant Jeanmaire was thus born a soldier's son and longed to be a soldier. He was four when the First World War broke out, and he has a clear memory of his papa standing in uniform beside the Christmas tree and of his great and good godfather Tissot, also in uniform, dropping in to visit.

'*Such a beautiful officer,*' Jeanmaire recalls of his godfather Edouard Tissot, almost as if he were talking about Deni.

Tissot was also beautiful without his uniform, apparently. When Jeanmaire visited him in his spacious apartment, he would likely as not find his godfather wandering around it naked. But no, Tissot was not homosexual! he cries in disgust, and neither was Jeanmaire! This nakedness was Spartan, never sexual.

Yet beside this image of military glory, Jeanmaire has a second and contrasting early memory that reflects more accurately the social upheavals of the times: namely of the Swiss General Strike of 1918, when the 'Bolsheviks of Biel' derailed a train in order to barricade the street, then hoisted the red flag on the capsized engine. Their violence against property and their lack of discipline appalled the young Jeanmaire, and his love of the Army, if possible, increased. Even today, given the chance, Jeanmaire would make an army of the whole world. Without his Army, it seems, he is in his own eyes a man of no parentage.

Jeanmaire is nothing if not the creature of his origins. For those who know Switzerland only for its slopes and valleys, Swiss militarism, if they are aware of it at all, is a harmless joke. They make nothing of the circular steel plates in the winding mountain roads, from which explosive charges will be detonated to seal off the valleys from the aggressor; of the great iron gateways that lead into secret mountain fortresses, some for storing military arsenals, others for sitting out the nuclear holocaust; of the self-regarding young men in officer's uniform who strut the pavements and parade themselves in tea-shops at weekends. They are unaware of the vast annual expenditure on American tanks and fighter aircraft, early-warning-systems, civil defence, deep shelters and (with 625,000 troops from a population of 6,000,000) after Israel the largest proportionate standing army in the world, costing the Swiss taxpayer eighteen per cent of his gross national budget—it has been as high as thirty—or 5.2 billion Swiss francs or 2.1 billion pounds a year. If their alpine holidays are occasionally disturbed by the scream of low-flying jets or bursts of semi-automatic fire from the local shooting-range, they are likely to dismiss such irritations as the charming obsessions of a peaceful Lilliput with the grown-up games of war.

And to a point, the Swiss in their dealings with the benighted foreigner encourage this view, either because as believers in their military ethic they prefer to remain aloof from frivolous explanation, or because as dissenters they are embarrassed to admit that their country lives in a permanent, almost obsessive state of semi-mobilization. For better or worse, Switzerland's military tradition is for many of her inhabitants the essence of Swiss nationhood. And the chain of influence and connection that goes with it is probably the most powerful of the many that comprise the intricate structure of Swiss domestic power.

To its more radical opponents, the Swiss Army is quite baldly an expensive weapon of social suppression, an insane waste of taxpayers' money, which recreates in military form the distinctions of civilian life. But to its defenders, it is the very spirit of national unity, bridging the linguistic and cultural differences between Switzerland's ethnic groups and keeping at bay the swelling numbers of immigrants who threaten to dilute the proud and ancient blood of free Switzerland. Above all, say its defenders, the Army deters the foreign adventurer. Just as apologists of the nuclear deterrent insist that the bomb, by its existence, has ensured that it will never be used, so supporters of Swiss militarism claim that the Army has secured their country's neutrality—and hence survival—through successive European wars.

Jean-Louis Jeanmaire—who still prides himself on having persuaded incarcerated conscientious objectors to change their minds—has subscribed passionately to this gospel since childhood. He had it preached to him by his father and again by his godfather Tissot. In the same breath they taught him the equally fervent gospel of anti-socialism. 'Good,' says Jeanmaire, meant 'patriot and militarist.' 'Bad' meant 'anti-militarist and socialist.'

But the small town of Biel did not at all share the reactionary visions of Tissot, Colonel Jeanmaire and his son. Its inhabitants were mostly workpeople. When the railway workers marched in support of the strike of November 1918—in the same days in which Jeanmaire witnessed the overturning of the train—the Army dealt with them swiftly, tearing into the crowds and shooting one man dead. But the response of Jeanmaire's father and his comrades, he says, was to rally a contingent of technical students to keep the gas and electricity works going, and arm the bourgeoisie against the rabble. Interestingly, local historical records award no such role to Jeanmaire's father, but say that the strike was broken by imported Italian labour. But whatever his father's contribution to the suppression might have been, his conservative posture did not make life easy for the young Jeanmaire when the time came for him to attend the local school. From his first day, he says, beatings by staff armed with sticks and the inner tubes of car-tyres became his fare. When he was unruly, the diminutive Jeanmaire was strapped to a school bench: 'I was the smallest but I wasn't the most stupid,' he says grimly.

Some boys in this situation might have learned to keep their opinions to themselves, or prudently converted to their oppressors' views. Not Jeanmaire. Always one to speak his mind, he did so more loudly, in defiance of what he regarded as the prevailing cant. Both at school and afterwards, he learned to count on his own judgement and assail mediocrity wherever he found it, whether it was above him or below him on the ladder of beings.

And this attitude stayed with him through his adult life—through the architectural studies on which he hurled himself with impressive result as a prelude to enlistment and into his career as an infantry instruction officer, which he pursued on the orders of his godfather Tissot, who told Jeanmaire that if he joined the Artillery he would never talk to him again.

At first, Jeanmaire's career proceeded well. In 1937, after the usual probationary period, he made instructor, rose to captain three years later and major after another seven. During the Second World War he saw service on the Simplon and in the canton of Wallis, and in 1956 he was made lieutenant-colonel and given his first regiment.

Yet throughout his steady rise, Jeanmaire's reputation as a big-mouth would not go away, as his Army record testifies in its otherwise quite favourable account of him: Jeanmaire was 'intelligent, lively,' but spoke 'too much and too soon.' In his work as an infantry instructor, he 'lacked respect and picked quarrels with his superiors.' He was 'qualified technically but not personally' to command a training school. On one occasion, in 1952, he was even given eight days' punishment arrest 'for insulting officers of a battalion placed under his command' during manoeuvres—though according to Jeanmaire, all he did was tick off a Member of Parliament for not wearing his helmet and call a machine-gunner an arse-hole for nearly mowing down a group of spectators.

True, Jeanmaire had his supporters, even if their admiration of him was played down in the Army's self-serving portrait of his inadequacies. To some of his superiors, he was a capable officer,

---

Opposite: Jeanmaire, having recently been promoted to major, in 1943.

an inspiration to his men, energetic, good fun. Nevertheless, the abiding impression is of a man impatient of fools, pressing too hard against the limitations of his rank and professional scope. At best, he comes over as a kind of miniature Swiss Lee Kwan Yew, thrusting to express great visions in a country too small to contain them.

Jeanmaire's accusers, of course, had every reason to present his military career in a poor light, for they were stuck for a motive. They had looked high and low for the thirty pieces of silver, but all they had found was a handful of small change. And not even the most implacable of Jeanmaire's enemies could pin secret communist sympathies on him.

So finally they fixed upon Jeanmaire's transfer to Air Defence in 1956 as the moment of his turning; followed by his being passed over, in 1962, for the appointment as Chief of Air Defence and Territorial Services, obliging him to wait another seven years, by which time the two responsibilities had been separated, and Jeanmaire got Air Defence only. Jeanmaire, it was reasoned, was 'disappointed and traumatized', first to leave the glorious infantry for the unregarded pastures of Air Defence, then to see a lesser man promoted over him. Jeanmaire denies this adamantly: perhaps too adamantly. The Army had always been good to him, he insists; he had status, and he was on the guest list for Bern's diplomatic round of military and service attachés; and in 1969, when he finally made it to brigadier, he got his apartment in Bern as well.

And he had a wife, of whom he still says little, except that she was the soul of loyalty and faithful to the end; and that she was beautiful, which indeed she was; and that he lights a candle to her memory each day.

The Army matters to Jeanmaire above everything. Even today. Even when he lay in the deepest pit of his misfortune, his faith in it burned on. He was in prison awaiting trial when, on 7 October 1976, Kurt Furgler, the Swiss Federal Minister of Justice, rose in Parliament to denounce the 'treasonable activities' of Jeanmaire, his 'disgraceful attitude' and his betrayal of 'most secret documents relating to war mobilization plans.' The next day, Switzerland's most strident tabloid, *Blick*, branded Jeanmaire 'Traitor of the Century' in banner headlines and ran photographs of the villain and his accuser on the front page. Three months later, the Federal President Rudolf Gnägi, addressing a meeting of his own party, confessed his deep disappointment that 'such base actions could be committed by such a high officer,' and demanded 'the full severity of the law.' There are Western countries where such words would have rendered a trial impossible, but Switzerland is not among them. The Swiss may have signed the European Declaration of Human Rights, but they have no law that prevents the public pre-judgement of those awaiting trial. Furgler also denounced Jeanmaire's wife, stating that she had knowledge of her husband's treasonable activities and in the early years had assisted him. (The charges against Frau Jeanmaire were eventually dismissed.) The Swiss insurance company Winterthur, from which the Jeanmaires had rented their apartment, also preferred not to await the verdict of the military court, but gave them notice, forcing his wife on to the street.

Yet among all these calculated humiliations, what hurt him most and hurts him this evening is that *his beloved Army*, also before his trial, caused his pension to be withdrawn 'in eternity'. The reason, according to one reputable paper of the day, was *Volkszorn*, popular fury. 'Our offices were exposed to pressure by angry citizens. A flood of letters demanded that Jeanmaire be paid no further money,' a spokesman for the federal pensions agency explained.

For a moment, it is as if the pale baby eyes are presuming to weep without his permission. They fill, they are about to brim over. But the old soldier talks brusquely on, and the tears dare not fall.

'That was a crime as never before,' he says.

'In prison I was never a slave but I obeyed!' Jeanmaire declares, hastening once more to the defence of old friends: 'No, no, they were good fellows, my fellow prisoners! I never had a bad scene! I was never set upon or insulted for what I was supposed to have done. I never felt threatened by a single one of the prisoners I met! I always made a point of warning the

23

Blick

UNABHÄNGIGE SCHWEIZER TAGESZEITUNG

Freitag, 8. Oktober 1976 — 60 Rp.

Nr. 235 AZ Zürich Tel. 01 / 36 36 36 18. Jg. 400 Lire ★

Jeanmaire

● **Auf Seite 3: So geht es weiter**

● **Seite 9: Folgen auch für Gnägi?**

Der Verräter des Jahrhunderts

VON KARL VÖGELI

BERN — Informationen über Kriegsmobilmachung, Organisation für Gesamtverteidigung und persönliche Verhältnisse von Politikern und Militärs: Alt-Brigadier Jean-Louis Jeanmaire (66) hat den Sowjets alles, alles verraten, was er wusste! Das musste gestern ein bleicher und sichtlich mitgenommener Justiz-minister Furgler den geschockten Parlamentariern mitteilen.

14 Jahre lang, genau seit 1962, hat Jean-Louis Jeanmaire Angehörigen der Sowjetbotschaft in Bern militärische Informationen geliefert.

Dubel war er nicht allein: Verrat wurde offensichtlich ein Familien betrieben. Denn es steht fest, betonte

Dass sie nicht auch verhaftet wurde, hat sie ihrer angeschlagenen Gesundheit zu verdanken.

Bleich verlas Bundesrat Furgler, von seiner Wahl in die Landesregierung selber auch Brigadier, den verheerenden Katalog von Verrat, begangen in vierzehn langen

Auswerkauf ihrer Truppenzeitung.

● Er lieferte Reglemente und Unterlagen verschiedenster Art bis zur Gliederung der einzelnen Einheiten ab, begleitet von handschriftlichen Erklärungen und mündlichen Informationen.

● Er lieferte Unterlagen über die Territorialzonen und die Organisation für Gesamtverteilung.

● Aus dem Bereich der Kriegsmobilmachung übermittelte der Meisterspion geheimste Unterlagen und Informationen.

● Jeanmaire beging noch politischen Nachrichtendienst, nicht nur militärischen Verrat; er orientierte die Sowjets über verschiedene hohe Politiker und Militärführer, wobei er Angaben über Charakter und Familienverhältnisse machte.

Dabei unterdrückt Furgler, dass er noch keine Detailangaben machen könne, weil die Untersuchung noch nicht abgeschlossen sei. Obwohl noch weitere «Ueber-raschungen» auftreten könnten, sei dem Justizchef klar: Zustände für die Beurteilung des Verbrechens wird von Militärgericht, wobei es aber noch nicht klar ist, ob ein übliches Divisionsgericht damit beauftragt wird.

Die Todesstrafe für den Verräter und «Lump» Jeanmaire forderte letzte Woche ein Basler Nationalrat. Wir sind nicht für die Todesstrafe, in keinem Fall, aber man wird für die

Jetzt heisst es handeln!

Empörung und die Enttäuschung, die hinter dieser Forderung stehen, Verständnis haben.

Jetzt erst recht, nachdem wirklich herausgestellt hat, dass Jeanmaire wirklich die geheimsten Dinge verraten hat.

Aber: Nicht die Diskussion um die Bestrafung des

Verräters, nicht die Suche nach allfälligen Mitschuldigen und nicht ein allgemeines Misstrauen gegenüber der Armee und seiner Leitung helfen uns jetzt aus der Patsche.

Jetzt gilt es, die Folgen des Verrates so schnell wie möglich zu beheben und alles zu tun, damit sich ein solcher Fall nicht wiederholen kann.

Das aber kostet Geld, im Interesse einer glaubwürdigen Landesverteidigung und damit unserer Sicherheit darf uns das nicht reuen.

Das meint Blick

Bundesrat Furgler erlebte gestern seine schwerste Stunde im Parlament: Er musste die Räte über das Ausmass der Affäre Jeanmaire informieren.

Einziger fester Punkt im Sumpf des totalen Verrats: Geheime Absprachen zwischen der Schweiz und der NATO konnte Jeanmaire nicht an seine Auftraggeber weitergeplaudert haben, weil — so Bundesrat Kurt Furgler (52) — es keine solchen Absprachen gibt.

Sonst aber musste Furgler die schlimmsten Befürchtungen — die auch im BLICK zu lesen waren — bestätigen. Die Wirklichkeit dürfen 163. Spionageszene Fälle in der Schweiz seit 1948 übertrifft bei weitem alles, was sogar bisher-tätigkeit ihres Gatten hatte und das mindestens in den ersten Jahren Beihilfe leistete

Furgler, dass auch Frau Marie-Louise Jeanmaire (52) Kenntnis von der verbrecherischen Tätigkeit ihres Gatten hatte und das mindestens in den ersten Jahren Beihilfe leistete!

Jahren:

● Er gab seine umfassende Kenntnisse über die Luftschutzräumen und den verheerendem Ausmass an die Russen weiter. Luftschutzoffiziere sprechen von totalem

Lesen Sie bitte weiter auf Seite 3

young ones of the perils of prison. I was a father to them.'

Seated at his little table, eating his fondue, we become cell-mates, sharing our hoarded rations by candle-light.

He is talking of the first shock of imprisonment: the terrible first days and nights.

'They took my watch away. They thought I could kill myself with it. It's very bad to be in solitary without a watch. A watch gives rhythm to your day. When you are free, you go to the phone, the lavatory, the kitchen, the book-shelf, the garden, the café, the woman. The watch tells you. In prison, without a watch these instincts become clamorous and confused in your head, even if you can't obey them all the time. They're freedom. A watch is freedom.'

But Jeanmaire's sanity, despite the harrowing assaults on it, seems as pristine as the polished steel bowls he keeps from prison. He has an extraordinary memory for dates and places and conversations. He has been interrogated by a rotating troupe of professional performers for months on end: policemen, lawyers, bit-players from the *demi-monde* of spying. He has been interrogated in prison hospital, on what should have been his deathbed. Since his release, he has given interviews on television, to the printed press and to the growing number of concerned Swiss men and women in public life who begin to share his view that he is the victim of a great injustice.

There are evasions, certainly. You hit them like fog patches along an otherwise clear road: willed unclarities where he is being merciful to himself or to third parties. For example, when you touch upon the delicate matter of his wife's affair with Denissenko—when did it start, please? How long did it last, please? When did he first know of it and what part did it play in his collaboration? For example, the number of encounters he had with

Opposite: The front page of *Blick* on 8 October 1976—'The Traitor of the Century.' 'Former Brigadier Jean-Louis Jeanmaire (66)' the article says, 'told the Soviets everything, *everything*, he knew! That's what Minister of Justice Furgler, ashen-faced and visibly shaken, had to tell a shocked Parliament yesterday.'

his successive Soviet contacts, and exactly what information or documents were passed on this or that occasion? We are talking, you understand, not of the discovery of the H-bomb, but of how the Swiss people would respond to the improbable sight of an invasion force of Soviet tanks rumbling up Zürich's Bahnhofstrasse.

Most difficult of all is to pin down Jeanmaire's own degree of awareness—consciousness, as the spies call it—as he slid further and further down the fatal slope of compliance. There we are dealing not merely with self-deception at the time of the act, but with fifteen years of subsequent self-justification and reconstruction, twelve of them in prison, where men have little to do except relive, and sometimes rewrite, their histories.

Yet the consistency of detail in Jeanmaire's story would be remarkable in any story so frequently retold. Jeanmaire ascribes this to the disciplines of his military training. But the greater likelihood seems to be that he is that rarest of all God's creatures: a spy who, even when he wishes to deceive, has not the smallest talent to do so.

Under interrogation, Jeanmaire was an unmitigated disaster; the tortures of sudden imprisonment worked wonderfully and swiftly on such a thrusting and sociable spirit.

'There were moments when, if I had been accused of stabbing my wife seven times, I would have said, "No, no, *eight* times!" Again and again they promised me my freedom: "Admit this and you are free tonight." So I admitted it. I admitted to more than I had done.

'When you are first locked in a cell you undertake a revolution against yourself. You curse yourself, you call yourself a bloody fool. You're the only person you blame. You protect yourself, then you yield, then you enter a state of guilt. For instance, I felt guilty that I had ever spoken with Russians at all. I believed I was guilty of *meeting* them, even though it was my job. After that came the optimism that the tribunal would deliver the truth, and they encouraged me to believe this. I had been a judge myself, at fifty trials. I believed in military justice. I still do. What I got was a butchery.'

He is no longer alone in this conviction. Today, the witch-burners of fifteen years ago are feeling the heat around their own ankles. The belated sense of fair play which, in Switzerland as in other democracies, occasionally asserts itself in the wake of a perceived judicial excess, is demanding to be appeased. A younger Switzerland is calling for greater openness in its affairs. An increasingly outspoken press, a spate of scandals in banking and government, now lumped together as 'the Kopp affair' after the first woman deputy in the Swiss government and Minister of Justice who fell from grace for warning her lawyer husband that he risked being implicated in a government inquiry into money-laundering—all these have beaten vigorously on the doors of secret government.

The new men and women are impatient with the old-boy networks of informal power, and suddenly public attention is fixing its sights upon the most elusive network of them all: the Swiss intelligence community. It is not Jeanmaire but the 'snoopers of Bern' and the professional espionage agencies who are being accused of betraying their secrets for profit, of spying on harmless citizens, of maintaining dossiers in numbers that would embarrass a country five times Switzerland's size and of fantasizing about non-existent enemies.

And as the decorous streets of Bern echo with youthful protestors demanding greater *glasnost*, it is the unlikely figure of Jeanmaire, the arch-conservative and militarist, the man who for so long hated popular revolt, who now walks with them in spirit, not as 'the traitor of the century' but as some flawed, latter-day Dreyfus, framed by devious secret servants to cover up their own betrayal. In the next few weeks he will hear whether he has won a reassessment of his case.

Yet whatever the final outcome, the story of Jean-Louis Jeanmaire will remain utterly extraordinary: as a tragi-comedy of Swiss military and social attitudes; as an example of almost unbelievable human naïvety; and as a cautionary tale of an innocent at large among professional intelligence-gatherers. For Jeanmaire, by any legal definition, *was* a spy. He *was* seduced, even if he was his own seducer. He *did* pass classified documents to Soviet military diplomats, without the knowledge or approval of his superiors, even if they were documents of little apparent value to an enemy. He *did* receive rewards for his labours, even if they were trivial, and even if the only real satisfactions were to his ego. Immature he certainly was, and credulous to an extraordinary degree. But he was no child. Even by the time of his recruitment, he was a full colonel with thirty years of soldiering in his rucksack.

So what we are talking of is not so much Jeanmaire's guilt in law, as the price he may have paid for crimes he simply could not have committed. And what we are observing is how a combination of chance, innocence and overbearing vanity precipitated the unstoppable machinery of one man's destruction.

'My two great crimes are as follows,' Jeanmaire barks, his delicate fingers outstretched to count them off, while he once more stares past me at the wall. 'One, I had character weaknesses. Two, I had been a military judge. Finish.'

But he has left out his greatest crimes of all: a luminous, fathomless gullibility, and an incurable affection for his fellow man, who could never sufficiently make up to him the love he felt was owed.

To describe Jeanmaire's courtship and marriage is once again to marvel at the cruel skein of coincidence that led to his destruction. For one thing is sure: if Jeanmaire had not, in June 1942, fallen innocently in love with one Marie-Louise Burtscher, born in Theodosia, Russia, on 12 October 1916, and if they had not married the following year, he would now be living out an honourable retirement.

He met her while he was travelling on a train from Bern to Freiburg. She entered his compartment and sat down: 'Lightning struck, I was in love!' They talked, he chattered Army stuff, he could think of nothing better. She was working as a secretary in the Bern bureaucracy, she said; and yes, he could take her out to dinner. So on the next Wednesday, he took her to the Restaurant du Théâtre in Bern, and of course he wore his uniform.

Opposite: Marie-Louise Burtscher prior to meeting Jeanmaire. The soldier in uniform was her first fiancé.

'Thus began the great love. I don't regret it. She was a good, sweet, dear comrade.'

Comrade is the word he uses of her repeatedly. But it was her past, not her comradeship, that became the chance instrument of Jeanmaire's undoing. Marie-Louise Burtscher was the daughter of a Swiss professor of languages who was teaching in Theodosia at the time of the Revolution. So it was from Theodosia, in 1919, that the family fled to Switzerland, penniless, expelled by the Bolsheviks. The Professor's last days were spent working as a translator and he was dead by the time Jeanmaire met Marie-Louise.

But Marie-Louise's mother, Juliette, survived to exert a great and enduring influence on Jeanmaire—greater, one almost feels, than her daughter's. Jeanmaire not only undertook responsibility for her maintenance but spent much time in her company. And Juliette talked—endlessly and glowingly—of the old Russia of the czars. The Bolsheviks were brutes, she said, and they had driven her from her home, all true. But the Bolsheviks were not the real Russians. 'The real Russians are people of the land,' she told Jeanmaire, again and again. 'They're farmers, peasants, intelligent, cultivated, very pious people. My greatest wish is to return to Russia to be buried.'

Thus by the sheerest chance Juliette became another of Jeanmaire's life instructors, taking her place beside his father and his godfather Tissot. And her fatal contribution was to instil in him a burgeoning romantic love for Mother Russia and an even greater hatred, if that were possible, for the rapacious Bolsheviks, whether of Biel or of Theodosia. 'Juliette loved Russia with her soul,' says Jeanmaire devoutly. And it is not hard to imagine that, as ever when he had identified an instructor, he struggled to follow her example.

The marriage began in Lausanne and followed Jeanmaire's postings until the couple returned to Lausanne to settle permanently. In 1947, Marie-Louise bore a son, Jean-Marc, now working for a bank in Geneva. In return for her keep, Juliette kept her daughter company during Jeanmaire's absences and helped look after the child. The couple spent about one third of each year together—Jeanmaire was for the rest of the time with the Army. 'My wife never intrigued, was not vain. One noticed in her that she had begun life from the bottom, as a poor kid. She had no girl-friends. She was a woman who was content with her own company. She read a lot, walked and was a good hostess.' And he uses the word again, this time more clearly: 'She was less a wife than a comrade.'

And that is all he likes to say about her, except to tell you that his lawyer has advised him not to say any more, and that he, Jeanmaire, doesn't know why. It is quite enough, nevertheless, to set the stage for the appearance of Colonel Vassily Denissenko.

It is April 1959 in beautiful Brissago in the Italian part of Switzerland, and the Air Protection Troops of the Swiss Army are giving a demonstration under the able direction of Colonel Jeanmaire. All Bern's foreign military attachés have been invited and most have come.

The climax of the demonstration, as is traditional in such affairs, comes at the end. To achieve it, Jeanmaire has ingeniously stage-managed the controlled explosion of a house at the lake's edge. The bomb strikes, the house disintegrates, flames belch out of it, everyone inside must be dead. But no! In the nick of time, stretcher parties of medics have arrived to bring out the burned and bleeding casualties and rush them to the field hospital!

It is all splendidly done. Under cover of the smoke, Jeanmaire has introduced his 'casualties' from the safety of the water, in time for them to climb on to their stretchers and be 'rescued' from the other side of the house. The effect is most realistic. The distinguished guests applaud as Jeanmaire formally reports to his superior officer that the demonstration is at an end. When he has done so, Colonel Vassily Denissenko of the Soviet Embassy in Bern, delivers a short speech of thanks and admiration on behalf of himself and his colleagues. For Denissenko, though newly arrived, is today by a whim of protocol, the *doyen* of Bern's military attachés. His speech over, he turns to Jeanmaire and, in front of everyone, asks him, in jest or earnest, a very Russian question: 'Tell me, Colonel, how many dead men were you allowed for the purposes of this demonstration?'

Jeanmaire's reply, by his own account, was less than diplomatic: 'We're not living in a dictatorship here, as you are in Russia. We're in democratic Switzerland and the answer to your question is "None". I cannot allow myself a single wounded man.'

Denissenko makes no comment, and the party adjourns to Ponte Brolla for lunch at which Jeanmaire, still flushed with success, finds himself, thanks to the *placement* required of protocol, seated at Denissenko's side. Here is Jeanmaire's account of their opening exchange: 'So that there is no misunderstanding, Colonel,' Jeanmaire kicks off, 'I don't care for Soviets. I've nothing against you personally, since you yourself can't do anything about the mess the Russians have brought upon the world, both in the Second World War and in the Bolshevik Revolution!'

Denissenko asks why Jeanmaire has such a hatred of the Russians.

'Because of my parents-in-law,' Jeanmaire replies, now in full sail. 'They were thrown out of Russia in 1919 and had to flee to Switzerland. They arrived without a penny to their names. As a result, I've had to provide for them.'

And to this, Denissenko replies—spontaneously, says Jeanmaire—'That's a terrible story. I don't hold with that sort of behaviour either. You must never confuse the Bolsheviks with the Russians. The Bolsheviks are bandits.'

Jeanmaire is at once reminded of the stories told him by his late mother-in-law: 'At this moment I recognized in him a czarist officer,' he recalls simply.

As to Denissenko, he may have recognized something in Jeanmaire also, for he soon returns to the subject of the injustice done to Jeanmaire's parents-in-law: 'We ought to put that right,' he says. 'The property should be given back. And you should receive something by way of compensation.'

But Jeanmaire still presses his attack. 'And look here. What about that disgusting business in Budapest three years ago?' he demands, referring to the Soviet repression of the Hungarian uprising.

Once again Denissenko is quick to parade his antipathy to the Bolsheviks: 'I agree with you one hundred per cent. And let

Jeanmaire with US General Westmoreland, in Switzerland, in 1969.

me tell you something else. In 1966, a certain Russian officer will be coming to Bern as military attaché with whom you should have no contact at all. He's the man who organized the whole Budapest affair.'

And thus—says Jeanmaire—did Denissenko warn him against one Zapienko, who did indeed come to Bern in 1966, and Jeanmaire avoided him exactly as Deni had advised.

In terms of intelligence tradecraft, the horseman Denissenko had thus far achieved a faultless round. He had presented himself as an anti-communist. He had nimbly touched upon the possibility that Jeanmaire might be eligible to receive Russian money. He had left the door open for further contact. And by warning Jeanmaire against Zapienko, he had planted in him a psychological obligation to grant a favour or a confidence in return. Yet to this day, Jeanmaire seems unable to believe that Denissenko's moves were no more than the classic passes of a capable intelligence officer.

'He didn't prod. He put out no hints,' he insists. 'He was correct in all respects. He had a great admiration for the Swiss Army.'

The meeting over, Jeanmaire hastened home to tell his wife the amazing news. His words, as he repeats them now, are like the headlong declaration of a young lover to his mother: 'He's exactly what Juliette your mother always loved! A real, fine czarist officer! What a shame she's no longer alive to meet him!'

Jeanmaire was so enthusiastic about Denissenko that he insisted that Marie-Louise accompany him the next month to a British diplomatic reception at Bern's Schweizerhof Hotel in order that she could meet Denissenko for herself. So she went, and Jeanmaire hastened to introduce her to his discovery. Denissenko, speaking Russian, asked Marie-Louise whether she spoke Russian also. She understood the question and said no. After that, the two spoke German.

'She saw in him someone who, like herself, had been born in Russia,' says Jeanmaire, explaining his wife's pleasure at this first encounter. And then: 'You can never tell what goes on inside a woman's head. Otherwise nothing happened.'

Speaking this way of his wife, Jeanmaire is once more too dismissive, too much on guard. There is another story here somewhere, but he is not telling it—certainly not to me, but perhaps not to himself either.

Throughout that same year Jeanmaire and Denissenko met at several receptions. Marie-Louise, according to Jeanmaire, came only once. Sometimes Denissenko's wife was present—from Jeanmaire's account of her, a pleasant, tubby, not especially pretty woman, a Russian *babushka* in the making. But the axis was undoubtedly between the men: 'Deni was interesting to talk to and felt bound to me on account of the injustice done to my parents-in-law. Perhaps my wife was somewhere in the background of his mind. I don't know. At that time, nothing had happened.' And this is the second time that Jeanmaire has assured me that nothing has so far happened between Deni and Marie-Louise. How did he know? I wonder —unless he knows better? When *did* something happen?—and did he know then, too?

At one of these occasions, Denissenko suggested a lunch. Jeanmaire says that when he reported this in advance to his brigadier, which he invariably did throughout his liaison with the Russians, the brigadier wished him '*bon appetit*'.

The two men drove in Denissenko's Mercedes to Belp on the outskirts of Bern, to the Hotel Kreuz, Denissenko's choice. Over lunch, Denissenko first talked about the battle of Stalingrad, in which he had served as an air captain. He dwelt on the horrors and the heroism of war. Jeanmaire, the Swiss soldier, was thrilled by this vicarious experience of one of the great sieges of history. The conversation turned to the construction of the new Geneva-Lausanne *autobahn* through Morges and to the uses of *autobahn* underpasses as atomic air-raid shelters. Jeanmaire was impressed by Denissenko's detailed knowledge of the Morges terrain. Denissenko drank no schnapps and little wine—on account, he explained, of his heart. Jeanmaire drank more freely, but not excessively. This is a regular refrain of Jeanmaire's narrative. Other encounters followed through the next year, but it was not until a full two years after the Brissago meeting that the Jeanmaires invited Denissenko to dinner, as usual—says Jeanmaire—with the advance approval of his superiors.

Denissenko arrived by chauffeur-driven car, and he was glowing with excitement. The date was 13 April 1961. On the day before, Gagarin had become the first man to circle the earth in space. Deni's elation was instantly matched by Jeanmaire's. Unlike the Pentagon, which was having kittens at the news, Jeanmaire appears to have been thrilled by Russia's triumph. The party set off for Savigny outside Lausanne for dinner, and the evening was spent discussing the space race. The local police chief walked in and, at Jeanmaire's invitation, joined them for a drink.

Jeanmaire on principle always paid his own tab when he was out with foreign attachés, and he paid it that night. After dinner, the party repaired to a Bern night-club, the Tabaris, where Jeanmaire presented Denissenko to the manageress. 'I was proud to be able to show myself with this man. He was very presentable: always well dressed—we were in civilian clothes—discreet but well chosen. He was a Gorbachev. When I think of Denissenko today, I see Gorbachev. I experienced *glasnost* twenty-five years ahead of its time.'

Jeanmaire recalls that Denissenko danced with Marie-Louise. The drinking, in deference to Denissenko's heart, was again moderate, he insists. All the same, it was a long, late, jolly evening, and what is significant in retrospect is that Denissenko, the professional GRU officer, made no attempt in the months that followed to build on it. If he was setting Jeanmaire up for a clandestine approach, he was playing a long game.

There are several possible explanations for Denissenko's apparent reluctance to develop Jeanmaire as a secret source. The first is that having taken a close look at his man he had decided, with reason, that Jeanmaire simply didn't know enough to be worth the candle, either as a present source or as a future prospect to be directed against a better target. Jeanmaire was discernibly approaching his professional ceiling, after all, and it was not, from the point of view of Soviet intelligence priorities, a sexy one. Other explanations lie in the still impenetrable marshes of the Soviet espionage mentality. No potential recruit of the sort Jeanmaire had now become could be approached without detailed orders from Moscow. Even in the GRU, which never approached the KGB in professionalism or sophistication, the choice of restaurant, the allocation of expenses, topics of conversation for the evening—all would have been ordained in advance by Denissenko's Moscow masters.

And it is beyond doubt that any effort to shift Jeanmaire

Opposite: On the balcony outside Jeanmaire's flat at the end of May 1964. Marie-Louise is on the left; Vassily Denissenko's wife is on the right.

from the status of 'legal' to 'illegal' collaborator would have been preceded by a ponderous appraisal of the risks and merits. Is he a plant, they will have asked themselves, in wearying evaluation sessions? A man so forthcoming might certainly have looked like one. Is he a provocation to secure Denissenko's expulsion or sour Soviet–Swiss relations? Does he want money? If so, why does he insist on paying his own way? And if not, how is this passionate anti-communist motivated? The astute Denissenko had not, it seems, detected in Jeanmaire those vengeful feelings against his superiors that became such a feature of the later case against him.

And perhaps—because of the delicacy of the diplomatic situation—the GRU may even have swallowed its pride and called in the KGB, who counselled caution and delay. Or perhaps the KGB gave different advice: perhaps they said, 'Keep Jeanmaire in play, but slowly, slowly. One day we may need to fatten him as a sacrificial lamb.'

All that is certain is that for several months Denissenko made no move towards Jeanmaire. He spent much time in Moscow, allegedly on health grounds, and no doubt when he conferred with his colleagues at headquarters the pace and progress of Jeanmaire's cultivation were discussed: even if he can hardly have rated high on Moscow's shopping list.

Then in March 1963, Denissenko and the Jeanmaires got together again, once more for dinner, and the topic this time turned to a Swiss military exercise which had taken place a few weeks before. A friendly dispute arose between the two men. Denissenko, who appeared excellently informed, insisted that Swiss military planning leaned heavily on NATO support. Jeanmaire, as ever the champion of Swiss neutrality, vigorously denied this, and in order to prove that the Swiss integrity was still intact, he says, he offered to show Denissenko the organization plan of staff and troops at corps and division levels, from which it would be clear that the Army maintained no NATO liaison of the sort Denissenko suspected. The Army, of course, most

Opposite: The only known photograph of Marie-Louise Jeanmaire and Vassily Denissenko—on the Jeanmaires' balcony.

certainly did maintain such liaison and would have been daft not to, though officially it was denied. And Jeanmaire knew it did, but the organization plan did not reveal this. Ironically, therefore, what Jeanmaire was offering Denissenko in this case was not dissuasion at all but Swiss military disinformation.

But Denissenko in return seems not to have taken Jeanmaire up on his offer. Why not? Too risky? Or simply a warning from Moscow to lay off?

Three months later, however, Jeanmaire bumped into Denissenko at a cocktail party given by the Austrian military attaché and invited him to his apartment in Lausanne. Three days after that, in the company of Marie-Louise, Denissenko and Jeanmaire ate a meal at Lausanne's railway-station buffet, then went on to the Jeanmaire's apartment where Jeanmaire handed over a photocopy he had made of the promised document, or part of it.

The document was graded 'for Service use only' or as the British might say 'confidential'. Whether it should have been so graded is immaterial. Jeanmaire knew it was confidential, knew what he was doing and who for. It may have been a tiny journey, but at that moment he crossed the bridge. In every tale of one man's path to spying, or to crime, or merely to adultery, there is traditionally one crucial moment that stands out above the rest as the moment of decision from which there is no return. This was Jeanmaire's. 'I gave only two pages, not the whole document,' he says. It seems to have made no difference. A Swiss colonel, as he then was, had voluntarily and without authorization handed a classified document to the Soviet military attaché and Resident of the GRU in Bern.

Yet the evening had only begun. Jeanmaire seems to have entered a vortex of reckless generosity. There had been recently a rehearsal of Swiss military mobilization plans. Now Jeanmaire took it into his head to boast to Denissenko that Swiss resistance to a Soviet invasion would be more ferocious than the Kremlin could envisage. He showed Denissenko his personal weapons, including his new semi-automatic rifle. He took him on to the balcony and pointed at the neighbouring houses. He is red-faced and thrilled as he describes this, and that is how I see him on the balcony. 'If your parachutists jump on to that tennis-court, everyone around here will fire at them,' he warned Denissenko. 'Forget orders. They won't wait for them. They'll shoot.'

He produced the *Mobilization Handbook* which is issued to every Swiss company commander. He had it by chance at home, he says, in preparation for a lecture he proposed to give in Geneva. Its classification was 'secret'. The stakes had risen.

Who was pulling now, who pushing? According to Jeanmaire, Denissenko asked to borrow the handbook, promising to return it the next day, so Jeanmaire gave it to him. As if it mattered who was the instigator! 'Anyway the handbook was common knowledge,' he adds dismissively. 'Everyone knew what was in it.' But that isn't what the official report has him telling his military examining judge on 23 November 1976: 'He [Denissenko] vehemently insisted that I give him these documents. Alas, I was weak enough to yield, and I thus put my hand into a trap that I couldn't get out of. From then on the Russians could blackmail me by threatening to inform my superiors. I told my wife that very day that I had made the blunder of my life.'

But Jeanmaire now denies that he said this.

And Marie-Louise—what did she tell Jeanmaire in return? It seems, almost nothing. Jeanmaire admits that he had an onslaught of guilt after Denissenko left, and confided his anxieties to his wife: 'And *merde*, on Monday I'll go and get the thing back!' he told her. But Marie-Louise, according to Jeanmaire, merely remarked that what was done was done: 'She had no sense that anything bad had happened.'

And still on the same crazy evening, Jeanmaire showed Denissenko parts of another classified document on the requisitioning of Swiss property in the event of war—for example, the seizing of civilian transport for the movement of territorial troops. This time he refused to part with it, but made a list of pages relevant to their discussions on 'dissuasion'. A day or two later, at his office, he made photocopies of these pages under the pretext that they were needed for a study course for air raid troops. A lie, therefore: a constructive, palpable lie, told to his own people in order to favour his people's supposed enemy.

Why?

And on the evening of 9 July, he handed the stolen pages to Denissenko. A criminal act. It was on that occasion also that, in the presence of Denissenko, Marie-Louise proudly displayed to her husband a bracelet which she said Denissenko had given her while Jeanmaire was briefly out of the room.

'When I came back, my wife said, really lovingly, "Look at this beautiful bracelet that Herr Denissenko has given me." I said "Bravo." I made nothing of it, except that it was a beautiful gesture by Denissenko. If she'd shown it me without his being there, I might have smelt a rat. Today I know he gave it her at a quite different time. It was a gift of love and had nothing whatever to do with betraying one's country.'

Denissenko's gift of love was worth 400 Swiss francs, says Jeanmaire. Referring to it later, he raises its value to 1,200 Swiss francs. Either way, it seems to have been a horribly good bargain in exchange for Jeanmaire's gift of love to him. The evening ended with another trip to Savigny for a celebratory drink. It is hard to imagine what the three of them thought they were celebrating. With Denissenko's bracelet glittering proudly on Marie-Louise's wrist, Jeanmaire had just put a bullet through his muddled soldier's head.

W hy? Jeanmaire's prosecutors were not the only ones to hunt for an answer. Jeanmaire himself has had years and years of staring at the wall, asking himself the same question: why? His talk of dissuasion wears thinner the more you listen to it. He speaks of his 'character weaknesses'. Yet what is weak about a lone crusader setting out to deter the Kremlin from its evil purposes against peace-loving Switzerland? He says the information he passed was common knowledge. Then why pass it? Why in secret? Why steal it, why give it and why be merry afterwards? What was there to celebrate that night? Betrayal? Friendship? Love? Fun? Jeanmaire says Denissenko was a czarist, an anti-Bolshevik. Then why not report this to his superiors, who

Opposite: Marie-Louise Jeanmaire.

might have passed the tip to people with an interest in recruiting a disaffected Russian colonel? Perhaps the answer was simpler, at least for the landlocked Swiss soldier: perhaps it was just *change*.

For the novelist, as for the counter-intelligence officer, motive concerns the possibilities of character. As big words frequently disguise an absence of conviction, so drastic action can derive from motives which, taken singly, are trivial. I once interrogated a man who had made an heroic escape from East Germany. It turned out that, rather than take his wife with him on his journey, he had shot her dead at point-blank range with a Luger pistol that had belonged to his Nazi father. He was not political; he had no grand notion of escaping to freedom, merely to another life. He had always got on well with his wife. He loved her still. The only explanation he could offer was that his local canoe club had expelled him for anti-social behaviour. In tears, in despair, his life in ruins, a self-confessed murderer, he could find no better excuse.

So again, why?

The more you examine Jeanmaire's relationship with Denissenko, the more it appears to contain something of the compulsive, the ecstatic and the sexual. Again and again it is Jeanmaire himself, not Denissenko, who is forcing the pace. Jeanmaire needed Denissenko a great deal more than Denissenko needed him: which was probably what gave Denissenko and his masters pause.

After Denissenko's departure from Bern, it is true, there came a grey troupe of substitute figures—Issaev, Strelbitzki, Davidov. Each, in the longer narrative, presents himself at the door, uses Denissenko's name, appeals to Jeanmaire's Russian persona, tightens the screws, finds his way to Jeanmaire's heart and receives an offering or two to keep the Kremlin happy—or to dissuade it, whichever way you care to read the story. Jeanmaire's relationship with the GRU is not broken with Denissenko's departure to Moscow, but neither is it advanced. Were *they* anti-Bolsheviks too? The fig leaf seems to have been tossed aside: Jeanmaire barely seems to care. For Deni's sake he gives them scraps; a part of him accepts that he is trapped; another part seems to tell him that his recent translation to the giddy rank of brigadier should somehow exempt him from the unseemly obligation of spying. 'I thought: Now I'm a brigadier, I'll pack in this nonsense.' Yet he continues to enjoy the connection. He dickers like a scared addict, offers them crumbs, warms himself against their fires, fancies himself Switzerland's secret military ambassador, wriggles, warns them off, calls them back, sweats, changes colour a dozen times, allows himself one more treat, swears abstinence and allows himself another. And the grey, cumbersome executioners of the GRU, knowing the limitations of their quarry, and even perhaps of themselves, make up to him, bully him, flatter him, accept what is to be had, which isn't much, and show little effort to force him beyond his limits.

Yet it is the figure of Denissenko that glows brightest to the end: Deni who obtained him; Deni who, if charily, baited the trap; Deni who slept with his wife; who was so fine, so well-dressed, so cultivated; Deni with whom it was a joy to be seen in public. All his successors were measured against the original. Some were found wanting. All were reflections of Deni, who remains the first and true love. Deni was noble, Deni was elegant, Deni was of the old school. And Jeanmaire, on his admission, would have slept with Deni if he had been a woman. Instead, Deni slept with Marie-Louise. The desire to please Deni, to earn his respect and approval, to woo and possess him—with gifts, including, perhaps, if it had to be, the gift of his own wife—seems, in the middle years of Jeanmaire's life, to have seized hold of this affectionate, frustrated, clever, turbulent simpleton like a grand passion, like a fugue.

So it is only natural that Deni, even today in Jeanmaire's recollection, is a great and good man. For who, when he has wrecked his life for love and paid everything he possesses, is willing to turn round and say: 'There was nothing there?'

The love of one man for another has had such a dismal press in recent years—particularly where espionage is in the air—that I venture on the subject with hesitation. There is no evidence anywhere in Jeanmaire's life that he was consciously prey to homosexual feelings, let alone that he indulged them. To the contrary, it is said that after hearing from his defence counsel Jean-Félix Paschoud that his wife had had an affair with Denissenko, Jeanmaire at once wrote her a letter of forgiveness. 'If they had offered me a pretty Slav girl,' he is supposed to have written, 'I don't know what I might have done.' The story certainly accords with his known heterosexuality and his self-vaunted hatred of homosexuals, whom he identifies constantly among his former military comrades: X was one and Y was not; Z went both ways but preferred the boys.

In this respect, Jeanmaire is a product of the Swiss military patriarchy. Women, to this Swiss chauvinist, are a support regiment rather than true warriors. Men, as in all armies, are most comfortable together, and sometimes—though not in Jeanmaire's case—this comfort flowers into physical love. When Jeanmaire speaks of his mother or his wife, he speaks of their loyalty, their good sense, their stoicism, their beauty. He is appalled by the vision of them as victims, for he is their protector. But never once does he speak of them as anything approaching equals.

And when he speaks of his godfather Tissot—the sometimes naked, otherwise superbly uniformed soldier, who, according to Jeanmaire, had to relinquish his command for failing to promote the 'useful' people—he recalls as if it were yesterday the terrible moment when he learned that his idol was about to marry a woman he had kept secret for forty years: 'Tissot had always insisted that soldiering was a celibate vocation. I believed him! I believe him to this day! I was disgusted to observe the two of them embracing. A world collapsed because I had regarded him as absolute. Not that I suspected him of homosexuality, but everyone regarded him as a priest.'

In Denissenko, Jeanmaire seems to have rediscovered the lost dignity of his fallen hero, Tissot, and perhaps in his unconscious mind to have recreated the dashing self-admiring friendship between brothers-at-arms that existed between Tissot and Jeanmaire senior. There is something *accomplished*, something *destined* in the way he still speaks of his bond with

Opposite: Jeanmaire (on the right) with his godfather Edouard Tissot on a mountain hiking expedition in 1933.

Denissenko. There is a sense of elevation, of superior knowledge, of 'I have been there and I *know*.' And something of contempt that adds: 'And you don't.'

Oh, and how the two friends could talk! Between them, the beautiful Russian soldier diplomat and the squat little Swiss brigadier redrew the entire world. They put out their tin soldiers and knocked them down; they fought and played interminably: 'When we talked politics, I represented democracy and Denissenko dictatorship. Each respected the other's position perfectly.'

And here it is necessary to dwell—as a defence witness at the trial is said to have done—on the social poverty of Jeanmaire's life. Good fellowship had been hard to come by until Jeanmaire discovered Bern's diplomatic community. Partners of the sort he craved were scarce in the ranks of his own kind, and his reputation as a big-mouth didn't help. He found solace in the company of foreign nomads. To them, he brought no baggage from his past. In their company he was reborn.

And finally—if love must have so many reasons—there is the agonizing comedy of Denissenko's record of real combat. To the Swiss soldier-dreamer who had never heard a shot fired in anger and never would, who had come from a prolonged military tradition of bellicose passivity, the lustre of Denissenko's armour was irresistible. Not Jeanmaire's father, not even his godfather Tissot, could match the heroic splendour and the vast authority of a man who had fought at Stalingrad, and whose breast, on military feast days, jangled with the medals of real gallantry and real campaigns. No courtship was too extreme; no risk, no sacrifice, no investment too reckless for such an exalted being. If two souls were warring in Jeanmaire's breast on that night of his first betrayal—the one thrilling him with words of caution, the other driving him forward along the path of glory—it was the example of his unblooded cavalry forebears that urged him to drive in the spurs and not look back.

One episode, more than any other, reveals to us Jeanmaire's state of mind during the high-days of his honeymoon with Denissenko: it is the bizarre encounter on 30 November 1963 when Denissenko called on Jeanmaire in his apartment in Lausanne and, in a classic pass, tried to fling the net over him for good. According to Jeanmaire the scene unfolded in this way.

Marie-Louise is in the kitchen. Jeanmaire, with his customary ambiguity when speaking of her, no longer remembers whether she is party to the conversation.

Denissenko to Jeanmaire: 'I told you when we first met that I would like to make reparation to you for the loss suffered by your parents-in-law in Russia.' Producing a large envelope, unsealed, he holds it out to Jeanmaire. There is money in it. Jeanmaire cannot or will not speculate how much. Hundreds, perhaps thousands of Swiss francs. He remembers hundred-franc notes.

'It's a compensation,' Denissenko explains. 'As I promised you. A Christmas present.'

Jeanmaire takes the envelope and flings it on the floor. Money flies everywhere. Denissenko is astonished.

'But it's not for you!' Denissenko protests. 'It's compensation for the damage done to your parents-in-law.'

'Then pick it up for yourself,' Jeanmaire replies. 'I'm not taking your money.'

The first time Jeanmaire told me this story, he was proud of his behaviour. It should prove, he seemed to think, that he was doing nothing underhand—much as introducing Denissenko and his successors to the proprietors of restaurants should prove there was nothing clandestine about the association. But when I pressed him to explain *why* he had refused the money—since Denissenko had offered it for such ostensibly honourable reasons, to repair a loss that Marie-Louise had undoubtedly sustained—he altered his ground: 'I perceived the money at that moment as a bribe. In refusing it, I was admitting inwardly that I had done something impure. I didn't want anyone to be able to say of me, "He can be had for money." I never had the feeling that Denissenko wanted to trap me or pump me, but I didn't want to take his money. It was repellent to me. It had the flavour of a payment for services rendered. I didn't want him ever to be able to say that I had sold my country—although I knew I wasn't selling my country or even giving it away for nothing.'

It would be charming to know what Denissenko and his masters in Moscow afterwards made of this bizarre scene and how much sound planning went to waste at the moment when Jeanmaire refused to swallow such a sweetly baited hook. How on earth could the grey men of the GRU be expected to understand that Jeanmaire wanted love, not money?

'It amazes me that Denissenko could have done it to me,' says Jeanmaire. 'After all, he could have given the money to my wife. But probably he wouldn't do that, because it would have made a whore of her.'

One might suppose that after this uncomfortable scene, the evening would have taken on a sour note. The suitor had made his pitch and been repulsed. Time perhaps to withdraw and fight another day. But not so. True, there were some sticky minutes, but soon the talk brightened and turned to the reorganization of the Swiss Army which had come into effect on 1 January 1962. Jeanmaire produced a copy of the previous order of battle, valid till 31 December 1961 and therefore out of date: 'I reckoned that since he was such a good fellow, I would give him something so that he wouldn't feel useless,' he explains. And adds that he had been told by Swiss military attachés how grateful they were to be slipped the odd 'little bit of paper' to justify their extravagant lifestyle at public expense.

But scarcely is this admission made than he is once more making another: 'I gave him the order of battle because I'd already put it aside for him when the affair with the money got in the way. But then I gave it to him anyway, to show there were no hard feelings.'

But if the path to Jeanmaire's mind appears tortuous and paradoxical, it resembles a Roman road when compared with the devious route that led the Swiss authorities to his arrest and trial.

Opposite: Colonel Vassily Denissenko of the Soviet Embassy in Bern.

Photo: Ringier Dokumentations Zentrum, Zürich

Here is the Federal Prosecutor Rudolf Gerber speaking before the Parliamentary Jeanmaire Commission, whose task was to examine the affair and whose report, though widely leaked, is still secret:

On 16 May 1975, we received a warning to the effect that a high-ranking Swiss officer had had significant intelligence contacts with the Russians. The time in question was 1964. It was difficult to work out who it could be. We knew only that the wife of this officer had had relations with Russia during her childhood. Thus we came on Jeanmaire. An investigation was launched in about August 1975.

You don't have to be a counter-intelligence officer to wonder what on earth was 'difficult' about narrowing the field to Jeanmaire on the strength of this information. The number of senior Swiss Army officers whose wives had enjoyed a Russian childhood cannot have been large. Jeanmaire's contacts with Soviet diplomats in 1964 were a matter of Army record. He had been appreciated for them in the military protocol department, where enthusiasts for the official cocktail round were hard to find. He had been deliberately flamboyant in parading them to casual acquaintances.

Where had the tip-off come from? According to the Federal Prosecutor Gerber, only a few initiates know the answer to that question. The intricate game of spy and counter-spy commands his silence, he says: even today, the source is too hot to name. The chief of the Swiss Secret Service at the time, Carl Weidenmann, tells the story differently. From the outset, he says, the only possible suspect was Jeanmaire. He too claims he is not allowed to say why. Apart from such selective nuggets as these, we are obliged to fall back on rumour, and the hardy rumour is that the tip-off came from the CIA.

What did the tip-off say? Did Gerber tell the Parliamentary Jeanmaire Commission the whole or only a part of the information received? Or more than the whole? And if the tip-off did indeed come from the CIA, who tipped off the CIA? Was the source reliable? Was it a plant? Was it Russian? British? French?

Photo: Ringier Dokumentations Zentrum, Zürich

Kurt Furgler, the Federal Minister of Justice (on the right),
and Rudolf Gnägi, the Federal President, on 9 November 1976.

West German? Swiss? In the grimy market-places where so-called
friendly intelligence services do their trading, tip-offs, like money,
are laundered in all sorts of ways. They can be slanted, doctored
and invented. They can be blown up so as to cause consternation
or tempered to encourage complacency. They serve the giver as
much as the receiver, and the receiver sometimes not at all. They
come without provenance and without instructions on the
package. They can wreck lives and careers by design or by
accident. And the one thing they have in common is that they are

never what they seem.

In Jeanmaire's case, the provenance and content of the original tip-off are of crucial importance. And until today, of crucial obscurity.

After the tip-off—a full three months after it, and fourteen years after Jeanmaire's first meeting with Denissenko —came the grand-slam secret surveillance, like a thunder of cavalry after the battle has been lost. Jeanmaire's telephone was tapped; he was watched round the clock. He was probably also microphoned, but Western surveillance services have a uniform squeamishness about owning up to microphones. A ranking police officer claims to have disguised himself as a waiter at diplomatic receptions attended by Jeanmaire: 'I heard only trivial party gossip,' he told Jeanmaire after his arrest. 'Soldiers' chatter about music, alcohol and women.' Again the police officer speaks as if he was wired.

And after four months of this, the watchers still had nothing against Jeanmaire except the tip-off, and what was vaguely perceived, in Gerber's words, as 'contacts with Russians in excess of the customary level.' But what *was* the normal level, given Jeanmaire's celebrated predeliction for Russian contacts for which the Army's protocol department gave him humble thanks? By December, the watchers were worried that Jeanmaire's imminent retirement would fall due before they had a case against him. Therefore Weidenmann, the Chief of the Secret Service, in collaboration with the Chief of Federal Police and the Federal Prosecutor, decided to offer Jeanmaire employment that would keep him in harness. To this end Weidenmann summoned Jeanmaire to an interview.

'It would be a pity,' he told Jeanmaire, 'to let you leave the Army without first committing to paper your knowledge and experience in the field of civil defence.'

For an extra 1,000 francs a month—later, in a fit of bureaucratic frugality, dropped to 500 francs—Weidenmann proposed that the pensioner Jeanmaire undertake a comparative study of military and civil defence in all countries where the Swiss maintained military attachés. Jeanmaire was flattered, and the investigators had bought themselves more time.

'I suspected nothing,' says Jeanmaire.

On 13 January, Weidenmann summoned Jeanmaire to him again and, in an effort to prod him into a betrayal, arranged for him to have access, through chosen intermediaries, to secret documents in the possession of Switzerland's overseas intelligence service. Weidenmann testified later that his department took care to ensure that Jeanmaire didn't get his hands on anything hot. The intermediaries, of course, were party to the provocation plan.

As a further inducement to Jeanmaire, a small office was set up for him in no less a shrine than the headquarters of Colonel Albert Bachmann, who ran his own special service, known in Swiss circles as the 'Organization Bachmann', and for long the object of much wild rumour and public agonizing, most notably after a ludicrous episode in which one of its agents had been caught spying on Austrian (sic) military manoeuvres. Bachmann was also charged with responsibility for Switzerland's 'Secret Army', which would form the nucleus of an underground resistance group in the event of Switzerland being occupied by hostile forces. No Soviet spy or intelligence officer worth his salt, it was reasoned, could resist such an enticing target as the Organization Bachmann. The office was bugged all ways up, Jeanmaire's phone was tapped and Bachmann was duly added to the team of watchers. But alas the hen still refused to lay.

Chief of the Secret Service Weidenmann before the Parliamentary Jeanmaire Commission: 'He was kept under observation during this period, unfortunately without success.'

After another eight months of frustration, during which Jeanmaire's every word and action were laboriously studied by his watchers, Federal Prosecutor Gerber decided to arrest him anyway, despite the fact that, on Gerber's own admission, he lacked the smallest scrap of hard evidence.

But Gerber and his associates had something on their minds that weighed more heavily than legal niceties and cast a shadow over their professional existence. The American intelligence barons had recently served formal notice on Bern that Washington had no confidence in the ability of the Swiss to protect the military secrets entrusted to them. Vital technical information about American armaments was finding its way from Switzerland to Eastern Europe, they said. The Florida early-warning-system had been compromised. So had state-of-the-art American electronic equipment fitted to Swiss tanks, most notably the 'stabilizor'. It was also rumoured that the Americans were refusing to sell Switzerland their new 109 artillery pieces and, worse still, threatening to relegate Switzerland to the status of a communist country for the purposes of secrets-sharing, a humiliation that rang like a panic bell in the proud back rooms of Switzerland's intelligence and procurement services.

Never mind that Jeanmaire had not been admitted to such secrets. Never mind that he was not qualified in the technology allegedly betrayed, or that the Army had chosen to confine him to a harmless backwater without a secret worth a damn. There was the leak, there was the threat, there was the tip-off, there was the man. What was now needed, and quickly, was to put the four together, silence American apprehensions and re-establish Switzerland's self-image as a responsible and efficient military (and neutral) power.

One of Jeanmaire's principal interrogators, who also arrested him, was Inspector Louis Pilliard, Commissioner of the Federal Police—the same officer who claimed to have dressed as a waiter to spy on Jeanmaire at diplomatic functions. During Jeanmaire's days of 'examination arrest'—that is to say, in the days before he was even brought before a military examining judge—Pilliard, the civilian policeman, questioned him, according to Jeanmaire's secret notes made on scraps of paper, for a total of ninety-two hours. Forget the European Convention on Human Rights, to which Switzerland is a signatory and which requires a prisoner to be brought before a judge in swift order: Jeanmaire had already served 107 days in isolation and had another six months to go before his trial.

'You have betrayed Florida,' Pilliard told him at the end of October.

'You're mad,' Jeanmaire replied. 'I can prove to you that I

Opposite: Albert Bachmann of 'Organization Bachmann'.

Photo: Ringier Dokumentations Zentrum, Zürich

don't know the first thing about Florida.'

And indeed, on the one occasion in 1972 when Jeanmaire could have attended a demonstration of the Florida early-warning-system, he had sent a letter declining the invitation, which Pilliard to his credit traced. But if the charge of betraying Florida was now struck out, Jeanmaire remained in the eyes of his public accusers—and of Justice Minister Furgler—a spy of monstrous dimensions. Finally, on 10 November, Parliament ruled that all derelictions by Jeanmaire *and his wife* should be tried by military justice.

For Marie-Louise was also charged. While her husband was being bundled into a police car on his way to work, five federal police officers, one a woman, had descended on the Jeanmaire flat in the Avenue du Tribunal-Fédéral in Lausanne at seven in the morning to conduct a house-search which lasted two days. Their finds included Marie-Louise's diary, where she had recorded all meetings with Denissenko, and a television set of unspecified origin, but probably given to the Jeanmaires by Issaev, one of Denissenko's successors. The diary has since disappeared into the vaults of Swiss secrecy, but it is said by Jeanmaire—who helped to decode it—to contain an entry that reads, 'Today Deni and I made love.'

The police also descended on Jeanmaire's friend and neighbour in Bern, Fräulein Vreni Ogg, at her place of work at the Bern office for footpaths. Having seized her, they bundled her too into a car, drove her to a police station and released her half an hour later, having apparently decided she had nothing worthwhile to tell them. The media had another treat and her life was never the same.

S oon Jeanmaire was singing like a bird, but not the song his questioners wished to hear.

Federal Prosecutor Gerber again, before the Parliamentary Jeanmaire Commission, in a lament that should be pasted to the wall of every hall of justice in the free world: 'The nub of the

Opposite: Jean-Louis and Marie-Louise Jeanmaire during the winter of 1975-76.

Photo: Ringier Dokumentations Zentrum, Zürich

thing is this: in Switzerland we do not have the means to increase Jeanmaire's willingness to testify.' After lightning arrest, solitary confinement, deprivation of exercise, radio, newspapers and outside contacts; exhaustive interrogation; threats and blandishments—what other means was Gerber thinking of, we wonder?

Jeanmaire was interrogated principally by Pilliard, who was sometimes accompanied by another officer, one Lugon, Inspector of the Waadtland Canton Police. Like Pilliard, Lugon had taken part in Jeanmaire's arrest.* But others, including Gerber himself, had their turn at the interrogation—Gerber for four full hours, though the content of their discussion escapes Jeanmaire's recollection: 'He shook my hand. He was decent. I told him I was relieved to be interrogated by someone of authority. My memory is *kaputt* . . .'

It is *kaputt*, perhaps, because it was on this occasion— 8 September, according to Gerber's testimony—that Gerber read out to Jeanmaire the list of the confessions he had by now made and which later constituted the bulk of the case against him. It is *kaputt* because a part of Jeanmaire's head knows that, within a month of his arrest and probably less, he had confessed away his life.

Nevertheless, the interrogation seems to have been conducted with a signal lack of skill. Jeanmaire, after all, was an interrogator's dream. He was terrified, disoriented, indignant, friendless and guilty. He was then, and is today, a compulsive, non-stop prattler, a braggart, a child waiting to be enchanted. What was needed in his interrogator was not a bully but a befriender, a confessor, someone who could interpret his dilemma to him and receive his confidences in return. Forget your lynx-

---

*My attempts to obtain the first names of Lugon, formerly Inspector of the Waadtland Canton Police and presently employed by the Federal Police, and Hofer, formerly Commissioner of Federal Police and now in retirement, have met with fastidious rejection. After one and a half days of consultation, the spokesman for the Federal Prosecutor's Office has advised that 'the two gentlemen Lugon and Hofer wish no publication of their first names for commercial purposes.' The spokesman, Herr Hauenstein, valiantly declined further explanation. Rumpelstiltskin himself could not have been better represented.

eyed intelligence officer, master of five languages: one wise policeman with a good face and patient ear could have had him on a plate in a week. No such figure featured in the cast.

On day two he was visited by Gerber's deputy, Peter Huber, who stayed an hour with him and, according to Jeanmaire, urged him to embellish his confession: 'Herr Jeanmaire, your case is not dangerous, but you should admit to more than you have done, so that we can get the damage out of the way quickly.'

What damage could Huber have meant, if not the damage threatened by the Americans?

Jeanmaire then asked Huber why he was in prison and what had happened.

Huber: 'I'm not allowed to tell you, I can't. But there's been a big leak to the East.'

Jeanmaire: 'But not through me!'

Huber: 'Don't get so excited. Things aren't as bad as they appear. Just own up to more than you did.'

Exactly *when* Jeanmaire confessed to *what* is hard to establish without the help of official records and, presumably, the secret tapes of his interrogations. According to Gerber, before the Parliamentary Jeanmaire Commission, it was not till 6 September that Jeanmaire confessed to handing over documents classified 'secret'. But whenever it happened, Jeanmaire says he was tricked: 'Pilliard promised me I'd be sitting with my pals in the Restaurant du Théâtre that same night if I'd just say this and this and this. They promised I'd be let out, and the whole thing would be buried. They blackmailed me.'

But Gerber's dates for Jeanmaire's confession are precise, whereas Jeanmaire, from the moment of his imprisonment, was living a nightmare, as his own testimony now begins to show, for it becomes fragmentary, surreal and, in several respects, doubtful.

But here it is necessary to pull back from retrospective wisdom and pity the poor intelligence officers saddled with Jeanmaire's case. They too were being blackmailed, if only by the fury of the Swiss—this *Volkszorn*—and by the urgent wish of the administration to heap on to Jeanmaire's shoulders every real or alleged failure of Swiss security in the last decade. The legislature, as well as the executive, was breathing down their necks. Jeanmaire describes a moment when he was telling Pilliard, the Police Commissioner, how Denissenko had remarked over dinner in Belp that *autobahn* underpasses made good atomic shelters. Before the eyes of the astonished Jeanmaire, Pilliard then seized a telephone and related to Minister of Justice Furgler in person that Jeanmaire had talked to Denissenko about shelters and atom bombs: 'I was suddenly a nuclear physicist and a designer of deep shelters. He said nothing of the context in which we had discussed these things.'

Now, of course, Pilliard's call to Furgler—though it is one of several occasions when he paraded a close relationship with his minister—may have been a policeman's bluff. Pilliard may have been talking to the doorman. But Furgler's description of Jeanmaire as a grand traitor was by now a matter of public record, and it is entirely conceivable that, in democratic Switzerland, the Police Commissioner did indeed speak directly to his supremo.

In addition to these pressures from on high, the investigators were weighed down with a mass of case histories of high-ranking spies in other countries who had indeed betrayed their nation's treasured secrets: men such as Wennerström in Sweden, Mitchell and Martin in America, Vassall, Houghton and Gee in England. A sack full of precedents was already raining down on them through the established channels of Western intelligence liaison. It would be remarkable if the CIA and FBI, for instance, had not by now sent out their customary squads of 'experts' and 'advisors', each trumping the other with ingenious theories of conspiracy. In America, James Jesus Angleton had already brought the CIA to a virtual standstill with his theories of moles in high places in the Agency. In Britain, Peter Wright and company were up to the same game.

In such an atmosphere, Jeanmaire was naturally elevated to the upper ranks of the spies' pantheon, and the Swiss were in no mood to be told that *their* spy was not as important as other people's.

Jeanmaire has been watched and listened to for a whole year without success? Then he has been ordered to lie low! Trap him!

Smoke him out!

Jeanmaire has no known means of communication with his controllers? Then he's talking to them by secret radio! Strip his television set, tear his flat apart, look for code pads, secret writing equipment, microdot lenses!

Jeanmaire has confessed to handing over trivia? He's giving us chicken-feed! Hold his feet to the fire! Grill his wife!

Jeanmaire has cracked and *still* not confessed to anything of value? He's a hard nut, a professional soldier, work on him some more!

If Jeanmaire is to be believed, even his defence lawyer, Jean-Félix Paschoud, was convinced of his guilt—though no man who collects an eighteen-year prison sentence is likely to think well of his defence lawyer. Entering his cell for the first time, Paschoud, Jeanmaire says, shook his fist in Jeanmaire's face and cursed him to hell and back: 'What you've done is an imbecility! You're a complete idiot! *Nobody* goes around with Russians, shaking hands with them!'

Well, perhaps Paschoud did say that, though it is not proof that he thought Jeanmaire guilty. Paschoud, according to Jeanmaire, was a member of the *Ligue Vaudoise*, an anti-communist group of patriotic cold warriors, and Jeanmaire's flirtation with Russians may indeed have shocked him. At the terribly brief trial, Jeanmaire complains, Paschoud was more exercised to keep his client quiet than to obtain justice for him. But Paschoud may have had professional reasons for wishing to keep Jeanmaire quiet. Jeanmaire was frequently his own worst enemy, and Paschoud was arguing that the charges against his client were out of date, which made defence irrelevant.

Jeanmaire likes to paint Paschoud as some small Lausanne lawyer whom he had known slightly in the Army, but the larger truth is that Jean-Félix Paschoud is one of Lausanne's few lawyers of international reputation, and was, among other things, lawyer to Charles Chaplin and his family.

The trial was from Kafka and beyond. Spread over four days, it lasted some twenty hours—roughly one hour for each year of the sentence. As of today, no official record of it has been released. The detailed charges against the Jeanmaires are still secret, though they have since been pretty thoroughly leaked.

Months before it finally started, both the accused had acquired a smell of death about them. From 21 September to 5 October, Jeanmaire, with severe angina and galloping fever, had been confined to a subterranean hospital. Under drastic medication, he had twice refused the extreme unction offered by the nursing Sisters. The interrogation by Police Commissioner Pilliard had nevertheless continued. Pilliard had thrust documents in his face and challenged him to admit he had betrayed them to the Russians. Jeanmaire believes this was the work of Colonel Bachmann. On Jeanmaire's return to prison, Pilliard, playing the good guy, had brought him a bottle of wine and two glasses. Jeanmaire asked him whether he was mad.

Marie-Louise, partly crippled by a stroke, was deemed too ill to be imprisoned, but not too ill to stand trial. How she had deported herself under arrest is left to Jeanmaire to describe. At first, he says, she had admitted nothing. 'She lied. She wanted to save me. She was braver than I was. If I'd behaved the same way, nothing would have happened.' She also denied having an affair with Denissenko, but her diary betrayed her. Jeanmaire, the transparent liar, off guard: 'I never told them about it either.' And as he hastily corrects himself: 'I never even knew about it.'

The Tribunal was convened in the classical Palais de Montbenon, in a small court-room belonging to the cantonal court of Waadtland. Jeanmaire was brought to a side entrance under heavy guard and allowed to change into his brigadier's uniform, fetched specially from Lausanne. The one painting in the court-room portrayed the judgement of Solomon. The spectators comprised some fifty journalists and the same number of members of the public. Jeanmaire entered and soon after him came Marie-Louise, walking with difficulty and in pain on the arm of a wardress, who led her to a leather armchair. She wore a blue suit. The judges entered; everyone stood. After a warning that the court would shortly be cleared in the interests of military security, the clerk to the Tribunal read a brief extract from the indictment. This accused the Jeanmaires of having maintained 'friendly relationships' with two Soviet military attachés and their successors, and with a colleague of the military attaché at the Soviet Embassy in Bern, presumably the GRU Resident Davidov, their last contact, during the period before he was an attaché. The rest was broad-brush: the result of these relationships, said the indictment, was the deliberate and persistent betrayal of matters or objects which in the interests of national defence were kept secret. The maximum sentence for such offences was twenty years in prison.

There was also a reference to 'passive bribery', though interestingly no such reference appears in the thirty-five leaked charges published in the *Wochenzeitung* in 1988. And this is hardly surprising, since the total haul of Russian gifts received by the Jeanmaires in the fourteen years since their meeting with Denissenko, including Marie-Louise's bracelet, the television set and a pair of 'freebie' cuff-links given to Jeanmaire, amounted to no more than around a thousand pounds—hardly a proper recompense for 'the traitor of the century', particularly when several senior officers of Jeanmaire's acquaintance had happily accepted free shooting holidays in Russia, not to mention such customary diplomatic hand-outs as caviar and vodka.

Still in the presence of the public, Defence Counsel Jean-Félix Paschoud, himself a military judge and lieutenant-colonel of infantry, and his colleague, Maître Courvoisier for Marie-Louise, then read statements declaring that there was no reason to believe that the Jeanmaires had accepted money from the attachés or that ideological motives had played a part in their actions. Paschoud's attempt to invoke Switzerland's statute of limitations in relation to the accuseds' earliest transactions with Denissenko was held over until the Tribunal had decided whether their derelictions were continuous or merely repeated.

The public was then excluded and the detailed charges were read out. While this was happening, Jeanmaire says, he caught sight of his interrogator Pilliard, who was listed as a witness, sitting in the court-room. He drew this to the attention of Paschoud, and the Tribunal's proceedings were suspended.

'Monsieur Pilliard,' said the presiding judge, according to Jeanmaire. 'You are a witness in this case. What are you doing sitting in the court?'

'I am here on the orders of Herr Furgler,' Pilliard replied.

The presiding judge asked his colleagues whether they had any objection to Louis Pilliard's presence. They had none, so the chief witness for the prosecution, according to Jeanmaire, sat through the entire trial.

Marie-Louise was dealt with first. Though no reference was made to her affair with Denissenko, Jeanmaire insists they treated her like dirt, barking statements at her instead of questions. Particular play was made of an incident in which Marie-Louise had wrapped a military handbook in a chocolate box before her husband handed it to Denissenko. In a whisper, Marie-Louise admitted she had done this. Nevertheless, when she was accused of influencing her husband to pass on information, she became extremely animated: 'My husband knew very well what he was allowed to do, and what not!'

At midday, her examination ended and she was led from the court. The examination of Jeanmaire began. 'The tone was malicious and appalling,' says Jeanmaire. 'The Grand Judge Houriet was like a snarling dog.' From the Tribunal, Jeanmaire learned his motive: it was vengeance for being passed over for promotion, and nothing he could say persuaded anybody otherwise. Frequently the presiding judge cut him short. Frequently Paschoud did. Towards the end of the day's hearing, an assistant judge who had not till then spoken made an appeal to him. It seems to have come from the heart. Jeanmaire relates it thus: 'Listen, Brigadier Jeanmaire, you're an honest man, it's known of you. Now tell us in Heaven's name what you have done. Tell us the truth finally.'

'I've told you the truth,' Jeanmaire replied.

So alas, still no confession to betraying the Florida early-warning-system, or any other of the vital American defence secrets whose nature we are only allowed to guess at. The dreadful shadow of communist status had still not been removed.

On the morning of the second day, according to the Tribunal's press officer, witnesses for the prosecution were heard. The first was the doctor who had attended him in hospital. The prisoner, he said, was in good health. The doctor was followed by

Commissioner Pilliard, who spoke generally about Jeanmaire's awareness of what he was doing and his admission that the information he was supplying to Denissenko and his successors was probably being sent to Moscow: 'It was after all his job as a military attaché,' Jeanmaire was alleged to have said.

Before Pilliard left the stand, he was asked by the judges where the tip-off had come from that had led to Jeanmaire's arrest. He replied that he could not reveal the source, since Justice Minister Furgler had ordered him to keep it secret.

Defence witnesses—all selected by Paschoud, says Jeanmaire —tended to compound the mystery of the accused's personality, rather than explain it. They testified to Jeanmaire's stalwart character and challenged the suggestion that he had acted out of vengeance. He was 'jovial' but never 'drunken'. He could shock with his outspokenness and disliked pomposity. Under his coarse exterior lurked 'a sensitive, soft centre'. He was a virulent anti-communist. An attempt by Paschoud to submit favourable written testimonials from brother officers was dismissed by the presiding judge. 'Let's get on with it. They don't interest us,' he is alleged by Jeanmaire to have said.

For the Prosecution's final address, Marie-Louise was brought back into court.

Remember, please, that we still have only Jeanmaire's testimony and the official press release and rumour to tell us what took place. The Prosecutor emphasized Jeanmaire's high responsibility as one of the Swiss Army's few brigadiers and the commander of 30,000 men. He dwelt on Jeanmaire's weakness of character and described him as a man trapped by Denissenko's charm and cunning. He dismissed Paschoud's claim that the early derelictions were outdated under the statute of limitations, maintaining that they were part of a continuum. He demanded twelve years in prison, reduction to the ranks, expulsion from the Army and the obligation to pay court costs. For Marie-Louise he demanded a year in prison, but would not object to a suspended sentence.

At this, Jeanmaire's counsel, according to his client, broke down and wept. 'Paschoud had never expected a bid for twelve years,' Jeanmaire explains—as if his own emotions were suddenly of less account than his defence lawyer's. In the midday recess, Paschoud had come weeping to him in his cell and said, 'They want to butcher you.' Did Paschoud, a toughened lawyer, really weep? Did Jeanmaire? Was Jeanmaire, at that devastating moment, in a position accurately to observe and remember the reactions of anyone, even of himself? Men facing sentence— whether of life imprisonment or even death—are known to experience a whole scale of sensations, from despair to hysterical elation. As far as Jeanmaire is concerned, Paschoud broke down and wept, and that is the end of it. What Jeanmaire himself saw, or thought, or felt, is probably beyond description. Fifteen years after the event, he seems intent upon turning the description outward on to his lawyer.

Only once, apparently, has Paschoud broken his silence since that day and with Jeanmaire's written consent: in an interview to a Lucerne newspaper published in September 1988 Paschoud accuses Commissioner Pilliard of extracting signed confessions from Jeanmaire by inducements and threats. He describes the circumstances of Jeanmaire's detention under investigation as 'scandalous' and takes exception to Pilliard's presence—as court witness and *de facto* prosecutor—throughout the trial. 'That certain people act wrongly is no excuse to do the same to them,' says Paschoud. Jeanmaire betrayed only trivia, he insists, and did so in order to show the Russians that the Swiss were ready to defend themselves. He was not a traitor, and he was treated like a hunted animal. Oddly enough, reading the interview, one can imagine Paschoud weeping after all.

Marie-Louise's lawyer, Courvoisier, on the other hand, rose superbly to the occasion—thus Jeanmaire, thus the Tribunal's press officer and thus, obediently, the press of the day. He emphasized Marie-Louise's subordinate role, an argument readily acceptable to an all-male Swiss court, and her freedom from greed or ideology. She was today a different woman from the one Denissenko had seduced, he said. He quoted from *Madame Bovary*. She had seen in Denissenko a man she could admire, he said. And at the end of his speech, Marie-Louise—'very sweetly'

Opposite: Jeanmaire emerging from his trial, 16 June 1977.

Photo: Ringier Dokumentations Zentrum, Zürich

in Jeanmaire's words—asked the judges to exercise clemency towards her husband.

Still not recovered from his breakdown, according to Jeanmaire, Paschoud now rose to his feet. As he spoke, he choked through his tears, says Jeanmaire. On behalf of his client, he pleaded guilty, a course that had not been previously agreed between them: 'He had never told me how he intended to defend me,' Jeanmaire complains. 'He wanted to minimize me, rather than contest specific charges.' Jeanmaire gives otherwise no account of Paschoud's defence, beyond saying that it ended with these words: 'I demand that Jeanmaire be judged and not condemned.'

But the press of the day accords Paschoud a more impressive role and credits him with attacking the 'poisoning of public opinion, political intervention and certain statements by representatives of the executive which had influenced the general public against his client.' According to the press, Paschoud even mentioned Furgler by name and described his speech of October 1976 before the National Council as 'not in agreement with the Tribunal's understanding of the case.' Paschoud is also credited with saying that Jeanmaire had possessed no proper friends in Switzerland, and that he wished to prove to Denissenko that Switzerland's defence preparations were strong and effective. This appears to be the only occasion on which the Defence offered Jeanmaire's much rehearsed argument of 'dissuasion', which today is his main self-justification.

Finally, Jeanmaire added his own last plea: 'It was never my intention to betray my country. In so far as I have done harm, I am sorry.' The session was declared closed, and Jeanmaire was taken down to his cell. Press and public were re-admitted for the verdict. Jeanmaire was brought up again. The Tribunal deemed the prosecution's request for twelve years too merciful and awarded him eighteen. The extra six were to be explained by Jeanmaire's high rank, which added 'exceptional gravity' to his crime. Only 'mitigating circumstances' had spared him the full twenty. These were: the services he had performed for Switzerland, the positive feelings he had retained towards his country and the absence of any profit motive. The Tribunal described his true motives as: ambition, self-glorification and resentment. The charges against Marie-Louise were dropped.

If the grounds for the verdict are still secret, the reason for the massive sentence appears less so. The Tribunal had done what was needed of it. It had made a big spy out of a small one. Such a huge sentence must betoken a huge betrayal. The witch was burned, a great leak had been stopped and America need no longer equate Switzerland with a communist country.

It is late, the fondue is long finished and Jeanmaire has tired himself with talking. A leaden prison pallor has descended over his too-expressive features. He is a little tired of me. The old soldier has served his time. But he is my host still. One last schnapps while we wait for the taxi, and soon I will return to my grand hotel, and he perhaps to the lady companion who now cares for him with the same loyalty as her predecessors.

He is preparing an autobiography, he says. Those files stacked against the wall contain just some of the thousands of pages that he wrote in prison.

A pause, then unable to contain himself, he asks me: 'So, how was it?'—meaning, 'How did I do?' As if we who come to him should declare ourselves for the defence or the prosecution, leaving through the 'yes' door or the 'no' door.

For a moment, I am stuck for an answer. His courage and his age alone, these days, make an innocent man of him, and there is a grandeur in Jeanmaire at eighty that is its own virtue. But old age can be a different state. The sweetness of old men need not be the sweetness of their younger days, not by any means. And it occurs to me that catastrophe has made a special case of him, accorded him a separate redemption beyond the reach of human judgement.

'I just want to report what I've seen and heard,' I tell him lamely.

'Do that! Do that!' His eyes, as he wishes me goodbye, are once more brimming with tears, but whether of tiredness, or regret, or merely old age, I cannot tell.

So how was it? as Jeanmaire would say.

Only one thing is certain: he had no way of betraying what they wanted him to have betrayed, and no evidence

71

was ever offered that he had done so.

All he ever gave the Russians was peanuts, not least because peanuts were all he had. And until anyone can prove the opposite, eighteen years was a barbaric sentence.

What he *might* have betrayed, if he had had any real information, is a nightmare that, thank Heaven, need not trouble us. He didn't have it.

And no, he is not dead, not by a million miles. There are men and women a quarter of his age in every small town in Switzerland, or England, who are a great deal more dead than Jean-Louis Jeanmaire ever was. He is a lover and a striver and a dreamer and a frustrated creator. He is a humble braggart and a tender bully. Perhaps he should have stayed with the architecture in which he was trained and briefly excelled. Then he could have enraged clients, insulted city councils, triumphed, failed, triumphed again with impunity. Perhaps he should have been an impresario like the Jeanmaire who staged the burning house in which his own life went up in smoke. Certainly he should have stayed away from any world that had its secrets.

He was never made for the Army, even if he loved it. He was born to it and, like the good soldier he was, he set out to fight the non-combat wars he had inherited. As the Army began to weary him, he started to dream that there was another, larger destiny being prepared for him elsewhere. In Denissenko, he thought he had met it: 'He's come!' he thought—*he,* my destiny; *he,* my rainman; *he,* the door to the lives I have not led.

Was there really a big spy somewhere? Does he or she still walk the corridors of Bern, knowing that Jeanmaire served his twelve years for him? Jeanmaire does not think so, but in the Swiss press, rumours abound and conspiracy theories tumble over one another every week. The Russians engineered the whole thing, goes a favourite story: they had the big spy, they were buying his wares, and when he came under suspicion they planted the tip-off on the CIA and fitted out the little spy Jeanmaire to take the fall.

Accusations and cross-accusations between members of the Swiss intelligence establishment are daily fare: it was Colonel Bachmann himself who was selling the secrets! says one cry—no, no, it was Weidenmann; it was Gerber; it was Santa Claus; it was all of them and none of them.

And certainly, like the spate of espionage scandals that have entertained the British for the last forty-odd years, the revelations about the Swiss intelligence establishment in the sixties and seventies point to a swamp of private armies, private interests, private fantasies and startling incompetence hidden behind walls of secrecy.

But the Swiss, like the British, love their spies even while they hate them. In purging 'the snoopers of Bern' the Swiss are also purging their own age-old practice of mutual surveillance. And the new men and women mean to end all that. They want to give the Swiss back their joy in one another, just as they mean to rescue their country from its perennial fantasy of being a threatened bastion of sanity encircled by mad foreigners.

Somewhere in the soldier and patriot who is Jean-Louis Jeanmaire—though he would be the last man on earth to admit it—there slept a man who had become sick to the heart of being Swiss.

Postscript, 16 January 1991

Revelations about the Jeanmaire case continue. The most notable source of information is, alas, still eagerly awaited as I go to press—namely the second volume of the report of the Parliamentary Commission. Some of its findings are already current, if unofficially and in draft form, and shed more light (or darkness) on the questions I have raised.

Unlike Federal Prosecutor Gerber, the Commission sets the genesis of the affair not in May 1975, which was Gerber's date, but in October 1974, when the 'representative of a foreign intelligence service' was despatched to Bern on a special mission to the Chief of the Swiss Federal Police to inform him that a high Swiss officer was giving information to the USSR and that this officer was married to a Swiss woman born in the Soviet Union.

The source of the intelligence was 'a Soviet officer', but the draft report does not tell us whether he or she was still serving or had defected.

The tip was at once passed to Federal Prosecutor Gerber, says the report. At further meetings on 29 October and 1 November 1974, the same 'representative of a foreign intelligence service' referred to a list of some sixty persons suspected of contact with the GRU in Switzerland and dwelt on the sensitivity of his source, who was not in a position to expand on the information or answer questions. This injunction seems later to have been ignored by both sides.

The foreign intelligence representative's information pointed specifically to 'a married couple living in Lausanne in 1964, who for at least a year had maintained contact with Vassily Denissenko, Soviet attaché and GRU Resident in Bern, and afterwards with his successors.' Their GRU cover-names were 'Mur' and 'Mary'. The wife spoke no Russian despite her origins, said the source, and regarded French as her mother tongue.

Gerber's later date for the start of the affair—16 May 1975—is evidently a reference to the visit of a different emissary from the same intelligence service, which resulted in a 'stock-taking'—thus the report—'at which new spy cases involving Swiss

75

subjects came to light.' It was also on this date that the Swiss officials, in the persons of Pilliard and Hofer, handed the emissary a questionnaire designed to obtain more information about the *still unidentified couple.*

On 2 June another meeting took place between the same players, and the foreign intelligence representative produced a new document containing yet more details about the suspected 'couple'. The husband lived in Lausanne but worked in Bern. He commuted daily, probably by car rather than by train. He was active in 'air defence' and had visited France in 1964 to acquaint himself with 'air raid' installations.

On 24 June the Federal Police received a reply to its questionnaire, confirming that the wife of the couple regarded French as her mother tongue, while the husband at least spoke it well. On the strength of this, the report concludes, the Jeanmaires were positively identified on 24 June 1975, a full eight months after the tip-off.

The draft report also refers to a *second* foreign intelligence service which came forward and confirmed the information given by the first. The British then? We cannot know, any more than we can know whether both services were getting their information from the same service—in that trade, no rarity.

On one point, however, the report is unambiguous: Jean-Louis Jeanmaire 'never had access to top secret files.'

I last saw Jeanmaire on 16 January and mentioned to him that I had succeeded in tracking down Denissenko. He was living in Moscow, I said, but was presently in hospital with a liver ailment. I said I might visit him next time I was there. Jeanmaire seemed not to hear. He looked down; he peered round his kitchen. Finally, like a schoolboy who has been promised a treat, he gave me a radiant smile.

'Oh, you *are* lucky,' he said.

ALEX KAYSER
OF SOLDIERS
AND BANKERS

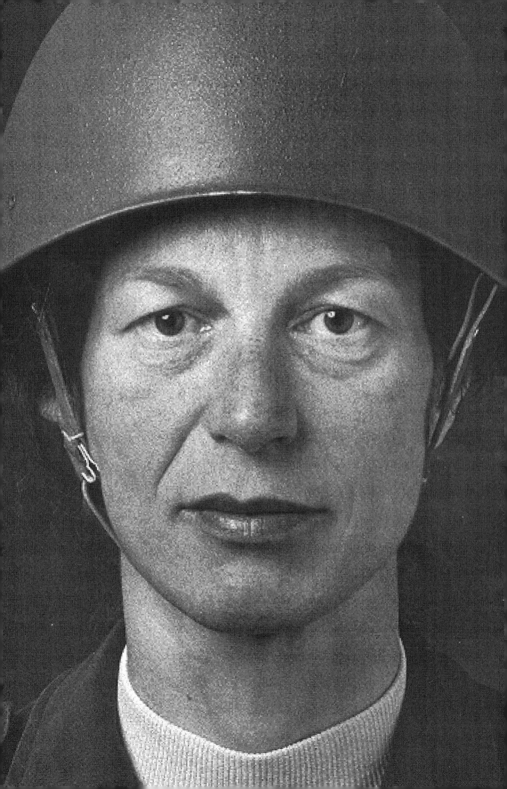

ROYAL NATIONAL THEATRE

MAX FRISCH

SWITZERLAND

WITHOUT AN ARMY?

G randfather, are you asleep?
—No.
—I asked you a question.
—I was just gazing into the fire . . .
The Grandson stands up: Shall I fetch another log?
The Old Man takes out a corkscrew: I thought you were joking. Switzerland without an army! It's not worth talking about. Why should Switzerland of all places have no army? It costs billions and billions, but we can afford it. We're a wealthy country.
—It's not a matter of money.
—Are you sure?
The Old Man uncorks a bottle: Would you like some? Then fetch a couple of glasses.
—They've collected over 100,000 signatures, Grandfather, so now there has to be a referendum. Even Parliament had to debate it.*
The Old Man fills the two glasses: And what did it say?
—That it was out of the question. That Switzerland couldn't manage without an army, that it was necessary for the defence of our neutrality and for our defence in general. A few outsiders, however, did raise the question: what was the Swiss army capable of doing?
—You mean, in a war?
—Of course.
—In a future war?
—Yes.
—And Parliament knows the answer?
—The top brass believes it.
The Old Man drinks: Are you still only a corporal?

---

* Anyone who has grown up in our region, no matter in which tax bracket, knows that we have democracy. I've known it ever since I could hear. In the state schools, in fact, it is believed that democracy was invented here, beside the Vierwaldstättersee. What is more, it is believed that the Swiss not only have democracy like other people, but direct democracy: not merely elections, but voting, year in, year out, and on top of that, there are plebiscites, and every true Swiss is proud that we have something like this to show off.

Photo: Alberto Venzago (Magnum)

—Yes, but they're putting pressure on me again. I got a personal letter from the major himself. It's the proper thing to do, he said. As soon as I've got my diploma I should enter the officers' training college.

—And why not?

—From a career point of view, you mean?

—Or do you plan to emigrate?

The Grandson drinks.

—Let me tell you something, Jonas. If ever the Swiss army is to be done away with, it won't be by a referendum, but by war.

—I don't know. To be honest, even if I do emigrate one day to America, I can't imagine Switzerland without an army.

—Who's asking you to?

—Dürrenmatt. He could imagine it.

—Dürrenmatt was a dreamer.

—What about you, Grandfather?

—Don't keep saying Grandfather.

—I don't understand your logic! On the one hand, you don't believe that the army is capable of defending our population in any war in the future, and you've said so in public. And yet you're in favour of my becoming a lieutenant, which would seem to imply that we should have an army after all, which we should go on arming—

—Logic!

—Teach me.

—The Swiss army is no threat to peace. Why shouldn't we buy German Leopard tanks or manufacture them under licence? It creates jobs. You must admit that. And why not American fighter planes? That, too, creates jobs. Jobs for guest workers as well. Without endangering peace—

—Yes, but without doing anything for peace either.

—Let me tell you something. Real peace would bring new dangers. If the images of our enemies were to fade, as would happen if we had real peace, the licences granted to armament millionaires would suddenly be at risk. It's not world peace, but only non-war that preserves the Swiss army from being abolished.

The Grandson stands up: So I should become a lieutenant!

—Why not?

—That's what I think, too.
—What do you think, too?
—That I could never be a threat to peace . . .

The Grandson stands in front of the bookcase, looking for something.
    —I'm glad you've come to see me, Jonas.
The Grandson starts leafing through a paperback.
—What are you looking for?
—Just a minute, Grandfather.
—I like to sit here by the fireside in the evening, when the embers aren't smoking. Our fireplace is far too big. They told me that in the beginning. Such a wide opening will never draw. You see, I took out the old chimney flue. It was covered in rust. And anyhow, we liked it better that way: a great big opening you can almost stand in. But they were right and it took me seventeen years to learn the right way to lay down the long branches so they don't smoke . . .
—I'm going to read you something, Grandfather.
—What?
—Are you listening?
—Yes.
The Grandson reads aloud: 'The contradiction that the army for the defence of democracy is anti-democratic in its whole structure only appears to be a contradiction so long as we believe assurances that it defends democracy, as I did indeed believe in those years.'
The Grandson shows the book title. —You wrote that, Grandfather.
The Old Man fills his glass.
—*A Soldier's Notebook*. 1974. Suhrkamp.
The Grandson continues to leaf through the book.
—Please don't read any more.
—Are you recanting what you wrote?
The Grandson reads out the passage he happens to have opened the book at:

What characterized a true Swiss then as now is this: there are certain things a true Swiss simply doesn't do; it

doesn't matter whether his head is pointed or round—
that's not what typifies him. The appearance of a true
Swiss may vary enormously. He doesn't have to be a
gymnast, a crack shot or a wrestler, but there is something
healthy about him, something manly. He may be a fat
innkeeper; the healthiness lies in his way of thinking.
Mostly he appears as a man of substance, or as a master
craftsman who has a right to demand that his apprentice
should also be a true Swiss. You don't have to explain
what that means to a true Swiss. He recognizes himself
as such. Even a poor physical specimen, capable only of
serving as an auxiliary air-raid warden, may be a true
Swiss. It has nothing to do with service rank; that's not
the point. A true Swiss is one even in civvies among his
friends at the café. Nor does it have anything to do with
income. The true Swiss may be a banker, but he doesn't
have to be. A caretaker may be a true Swiss, or a teacher.
And anyone who doesn't know what a true Swiss is
learns it during military service . . . Although there are
also true Swiss women, the true Swiss undoubtedly feels
more comfortable among men. That's not the only
reason the army suits him. It can't be said that the
uniform suits every true Swiss; generally speaking it
suits the officers better.

The Grandson laughs: That's a bit dismissive, Grandfather.
The Old Man fills his glass: Let's talk about something else!
A pause.

—Grandfather, at the outbreak of World War Two what
did you believe the Germans would do?.

The Old Man remains silent.

—Did people believe that after Hitler's *Wehrmacht* had
overrun Poland and Holland, and then France, it wouldn't dare
cross the Rhine and enter Switzerland because you were standing
there with your helmets and fixed bayonets?

—I was in Ticino.

—My question annoys you. Why?

—Because everyone knows the answer. It was a matter of

paying the price of admission. None of us imagined we were going to make mincemeat of the *Wehrmacht*, but defeating the Swiss army represented a price of admission that Hitler couldn't afford to pay.

—And that's how it worked out.

The Grandson coughs and laughs: Now the fire is smoking!

The Old Man stands up and opens the door.

The Grandson remains seated, leafing through the paperback.

—Do you mind the draught?

The Old Man shuts the door, comes back to the fireside and remains standing: Will you fetch us another log?

—There's still one to burn, Grandfather.

The Young Man continues leafing through the book: I didn't mean to upset you. I am sorry. Even in kindergarten they tell you it was our army that kept Switzerland out of the Second World War.

The Old Man takes the poker, bends down and rakes the fire and stops it from smoking.

The Young Man reads out:

When the news of the *Wehrmacht*'s victories first came over our radio, I was with a kitchen detail fetching cauldrons of soup and sacks of bread and I hadn't heard a thing. The troops came along angrily with their mess tins; they didn't want to talk; when we asked them, they merely laughed angrily and said the Germans were always great boasters. The quick collapse of Poland was a disappointment, but Poland was a long way away. Later, when Holland and Belgium collapsed even more quickly, the troops said Holland and Belgium didn't have mountains like us. We knew the *Wehrmacht* couldn't be stopped at our frontier; no one claimed that. To that extent we thought of ourselves as having no illusions. But we would fight. We didn't need to proclaim it. It went without saying, in accordance with Swiss history. And if we did proclaim it, our proclamations were not for us; they were aimed at Hitler, in case he was under any illusions. Otherwise why were we training day and night? France was occupied and suddenly the Germans were at the gates of Geneva. But we would fight, from defeat to defeat, until the mountains protected us. The new concept: the *redoubt*.

The Grandson goes on leafing through the book: When did you write this little book?
—Before Chernobyl.
The Old Man places a log on the fire: That's chestnut, it burns slowly . . .
He refills his glass: Jonas, you're not drinking . . .
The Grandson takes a sip: How high would the price of admission have been?
The Old Man takes a long draught: That's the best Jeninser, an excellent wine . . .
The Grandson reads aloud:

There were four pill-boxes. In meadowland, green and flat, an open terrain. An open, green tray, as seen from a plane: the four ochre-yellow construction sites in a configuration that gave the show away; the pill-boxes just finished, covered over by fresh earth, a cement-mixer still standing nearby. We didn't know much about the German Stukas but we knew this: they wouldn't have to hunt for long; four bombing runs would be enough. We would have preferred to have set up the anti-aircraft guns under the apple trees or, better still, in the forest nearby. But it wasn't up to us. Later, when I was alone with the captain in a small commando tent, I asked him what he thought of our position. A joke, he knew that at the time; we would have been wiped out before the guns with their limited range could have latched on to a target.

—Why are you reading that?
—I find it thrilling.
—Stop it, Jonas. Switzerland without an army is unthinkable. Our people have believed in this army since Napoleon's day.

The Grandson goes on turning the pages.
—Now drop it!
The Grandson reads out:

May 1940, during a night when we were expecting the German attack, a telephone patrol that had to lay a cable came along the main road from Zürich. There was a black-out and cars were travelling with dimmed lights, columns of private cars from Zürich. One of us stood in the roadway with a pocket torch and asked the civilians: Where are you going? We made a joke of asking everyone. They were pale and docile, nervous like people at a border. One of them had a summer cottage on the Lake of Thun; the next one had relations in the Emmental; there was another with a summer cottage and so on. Zürich will be defended, said our warrior with a heavy coil of cable on his back, that's what we're here for. The cars were packed solid with suitcases, bags, fur coats, even chandeliers, with rolled up carpets on the roof . . . I was indignant. But not the fellow with the torch and the heavy cable on his back; he was more realistic. They've got summer cottages, we haven't. That's all there is to it.

The Old Man laughs: That was in those days. A summer cottage near Grindelwald or in the Valais is out of date. If we were threatened now the leaders of industry would move into their luxury bolt-holes in Canada.
—Is that right?
—The Rockefeller clan has a bolt-hole like that, in a splendid location in the Caribbean. It's said to be radiation proof. The small part that's visible above the rock I've seen myself from a dinghy.
The Grandson stands up and goes to the window: May I?
He opens the window: What interests me, Grandfather—
—Which of us will go to Canada?
—No, Grandfather, I'm serious.
—That is serious. That's part of 'total defence': that the Swiss economy shall survive until Swiss territory is once more

habitable and a field for domestic trade.

—What did General Guisan say on the Rütli?*

—We don't know exactly. It's certain that General Guisan assembled the army top brass and announced that even after the fall of France our will to resist any attack remained firm. That was a historic event, indeed, on the historic Rütli meadow. But there is no record of what he said.

—No tape-recording?

—No.

—No notes?

—Nothing.

—Odd.

The Grandson closes the window and sits down again: Did you believe in the *redoubt* back then?

—You know, Jonas . . .

The Old Man drinks some wine (the Grandson has picked up the book again and seems to know which passage he is looking for) and then speaks: Hitler's army is outside Leningrad and Hitler's army is on the Atlantic; as a gunner you feel very relieved to be able to hole up on the Lukmanier or the Furka, which Hitler doesn't need. But how many winters can you hold out there?—when you know that a *Wehrmacht* officer is living with your wife in Zürich, two or three of your friends are probably in a concentration camp, everyone else is toiling for the Third Reich, while we stand fast in our position up in the mountains, defending the marmots. The *redoubt* was a brilliant idea.

---

* (Between 9 April and 14 June 1940, the German armies had invaded Denmark, Norway, Holland, Belgium, Luxembourg and France. Fifteen days later Federal President Marcel Pilet-Golaz made a famous, and famously inadequate, radio speech in which he announced that the military would be partially demobilized and that Switzerland should be prepared to play its part in the 'new' Europe. In protest, the commander-in-chief of the army, Henri Guisan took, on the morning of 25 July 1940, 500 officers to the meadow of Rütli, the birthplace of the Confederation of Switzerland, and, symbolically renewing the Rütli oath, supposedly issued the order 'to resist any attack from without and all dangers on the home front, such as sloth or defeatism.')

The Grandson is still leafing through the book; the Old Man continues: Of course the Allies would have kept us supplied. They had parachutes, and the Luftwaffe would have fought shy of our mountains. And we would have cheered each other on, while the enemy held the whole of the central area and the cities, the villages, the whole of Swiss industry and, as I said, your wife. But we, the men in camouflage, would have flapped our arms round our own chests in the cold and wouldn't have been starved out, and would have been careful with the ammunition in the caves and for years on end would have been convinced that we represented a threat to the enemy's flank—to the *Wehrmacht* between the Atlantic and Odessa . . . I don't know how long we could have gone on believing that.

The Grandson has found what he was looking for and reads out:

Once, in 1943, we had a visit from General Guisan. I had seen him before he was elected general, at a lecture at the Swiss Institute of Technology. Now he stood there in the snow: somewhat shorter than one would have imagined from the well-known half-length portrait. We were moved. There was no parade; he had come to see our ski training. Up above Samedan. He wore snow-glasses. We had to wait on the slope, ready for the start. It took quite a long time, but we remained moved. It really was him, Our General, whose half-length portrait hung in every inn parlour and government office. It was a cold winter day with sunshine. Each one of us had to ski a simple curve past the man who was already part of Swiss history, no big deal on good snow, and the snow was good.

—You find that dismissive?
—That's not the passage I meant . . .
—That was before Stalingrad.

The Grandson finds the passage and reads it out: 'On 14.8.1940, that is to say barely a month after the Rütli speech, General Guisan requested that a delegation led by Minister C. J. Burckhardt should be sent to Berlin *"pour tenter un apaisement et instituer une collaboration."* The Federal Council rejected the

request.'
—There you are.
—Did the General believe in his *redoubt*?
The Grandson puts away the paperback: Now it's hardly smoking at all.
—Because there's a flame.
—Do you remember the sergeant-major you mentioned in this book, in May 1940, when you were expecting the invasion?
—I wonder if he's still alive?
—Did he ever read your book?
—We liked him.
—So you write.
—He was a farmer, I think, from Bern, stronger than any of us, an ox: he took hold of the spokes with his own hands when the going was too steep . . . I remember how he stood that evening behind the barn. Roll-call in the afternoon, that was unusual. Our captain said the German invasion would probably take place at four in the morning. So shave and rest. No trips to the inn. So stand-by. So we stood around waiting, except for the two drivers, who took their cars and slipped off to Zürich to see their wives. It was still too early to sleep in the barn. Too bright, too beautiful: the meadows, the chickens, the flowering trees. And as he had been standing off to one side for an hour, I went up to him. I don't know whether he even heard me. After a while he said: If they come I'll shoot myself!
—Do you think he'd have done it?
The Old Man laughs briefly: It was a solemn moment, yes—
—What do you mean?
—I was sitting on a concrete pipe under a small apple tree, my elbows on my knees, gazing out at the ploughed field. So this was where it was all going to end. What came into my mind? The sea.
The Old Man fills his glass.
—But you think the army would have fought.
—Sure, yes, most of it.
The Old Man does not drink but reflects: My brother was a first lieutenant. A young chemist, a PhD. You can't get anywhere at SANDOZ or GEIGY as a gunner. And Franz had to look after

our mother. Moreover, he had health problems, but he wanted to do his military service. Franz as an officer! His wife was a Polish Jewess. Did you ever meet her? His battery had modern howitzers, unlike ours.* It was only later, much later, after the victory of the victorious powers, that he told me that up to 1943, that's to say Stalingrad, there was absolutely no agreement, if things went that far, to allow the two batteries to fire. Many of the officers were by no means unsympathetic to many aspects of Hitler's Germany. There would have been eight howitzers in a perfect location and no one knew who would have held back when the trouble started.

The Old Man empties his glass: Our battery on the Mutschellen would have fought, of that I'm sure, at least until the first German Stuka attack later in the morning.

A pause.

—When did you first hear about the concentration camps?

The Old Man reaches for the paperback: It's in here, I think.

The Old Man leafs through it: Where did I put my glasses?

—I thought you didn't want to hear any more from this little book.

The Old Man finds his glasses: It's in here somewhere.

The Old Man turns the pages this way and that: At the time I missed the address to the Swiss people (25.6.1940) by a Swiss Federal President whose neutral gaze was already far-sightedly directed towards Adolf Hitler's New Europe . . .

The Old Man turns more pages: His name was Pilet-Golaz . . .

---

*Our battery, designated as a motorized mountain artillery unit, had field guns dating from 1903. Since they had no rubber tyres, the guns could not be towed by motor vehicles but had to be loaded on to motor vehicles, which could be done by the muscle power of eight gunners, but took a long time. And since we were not stationed on the Marne with these field cannons, but in Ticino or the Engadine, in order to fire over the top of our own mountains, we had always to mount them on trestles; first, of course, we had to flatten the ground, so that these trestles had a firm foundation and didn't tip over at the first shot. We also had the vague idea that the enemy would have plenty of time to shell us while we were still setting up these trestles every time we moved our position.

—And you complain about your memory!

The Old Man reads aloud: '30.8.1942. After three years of war there are 9,600 refugees in Switzerland. Federal Councillor von Steiger, responsible for Swiss policy on refugees, declared before a local congregation of the Young Church: 'The boat is full.'

—I've heard about that.

—Nine thousand six hundred, the same number as at a second division soccer match.

The Old Man reads aloud: '9.1.1944. Edda Ciano, Mussolini's daughter, crosses the Swiss border illegally with her children. She is refused asylum, but does not leave the country until after the war.'

—Not from a Kurdish family, then.

The Old Man continues: '6.2.1945. The Federal Council protests to the German Government about the mass murder of Jews and permits the entry of 1,200 Jewish inmates from Theresienstadt concentration camp.'

The Old Man stops: We saw some of them, arriving at Schuls Railway Station. Our medical orderlies gave them hot soup, or at least they tried to. In some cases it ran straight through them into their prison trousers.

The Old Man turns more pages and reads out: 'As far as the refugees were concerned, we were never told the criteria by which some were given asylum and others turned back at the border. Our job was to be fit to march and to know how to look after our marching boots even when on leave.'

The Old Man closes the book sharply: I can't find the passage!

He stands up and replaces the book on the shelf: Memory, Jonas, memory!

—It fades, you tell me.

—On the contrary, Jonas . . . I was with an old Swiss friend—he is also seventy now—in the Tobelhof recently and over liver sausage and sauerkraut, he suddenly told me what he had seen as a lance-corporal from his post on one of the Rhine bridges. We've known one another for thirty years—I've occasionally stayed with him—but Gottfried never told me anything about his time in the army. And now suddenly out of the blue he described watching from his post as a few more Jews tried to escape the SS by swimming the Rhine. The Rhine is no brook outside Basel; a Walter Benjamin would never have reached the first pier, nor little Anne Frank. But one of them managed it that night. Almost unbelievable. He wasn't swept away by the swirling brown water like all the rest, but was able to hang on, and he thought that he was saved. Of course he knew: CROSSING STRICTLY FORBIDDEN. And Gottfried, as an unarmed medical orderly, watched and didn't have to shoot. And this obviously gave the Jew fresh strength: he actually managed to reach the Swiss river-bank, where he was able to cling to some projection with one hand. For a while, said Gottfried. And then a lieutenant came along, a Swiss that is, who knew his orders and trod on the four clinging fingers with the heel of his boot—splash, he was gone! The young Jew must have drowned, before the Rhine became a German river.

The Old Man sits down by the fireside again: Let's talk about something else!

The Grandson fills his glass: Is it true, Grandfather, that you no longer write? Apart from letters. I mean, no novels, and so on. No journal?

—That's been true for years.

—You never wrote poetry?

The Old Man shrugs his shoulders and says nothing.

—Just listen to that rain!

The Old Man declaims:

Do you think Zürich, for example,
is a city more profound,
where miracles and magic
are always to be found?

—Did you write that?

—Gottfried Benn.

—When you were still able to go for hikes, I remember, there was one hike on which you recited half of Brecht to my father.

105

—That must have been a long hike.
—It seemed long to me.
The Old Man declaims:

When he was seventy, of strength bereft,
The old man longed for rest
For goodness in the land was wasting away
And evil growing stronger by the day
So he upped and left.

—That's Brecht.
—More or less.
—Do you know many more poems by heart?
—Fewer and fewer.
The Old Man declaims:

He will be decorated
for desertion from the colours
for courage in the face of the friend . . .

He falters: But how does it start? A star as a medal that someone is awarded, the wretched star of hope over heart . . . The Old Man declaims:

He will be decorated
for courage in the face of the friend
for betraying shameful secrets
and disregarding
every order.

—That sounds pretty radical.
—Ingeborg Bachman.
—Has it been published?
A pause.
—What do you do when you can't do anything in the garden, because it's raining, and there's nothing on TV but Swiss programmes?
—I read . . .
The Grandson spots a book on the mantelpiece: Denis Diderot?
—For example.

The Old Man takes a newspaper out of the basket: And newspapers, yes, them too.

The Old Man reads aloud: 'At thirty per cent, suicide is the most frequent cause of death among Swiss men between twenty and thirty-four . . . Scientists attribute the increase in the suicide rate among the young above all to the increased pressure to conform . . . In addition young people today experience a greater fear of being unable to fit into society.'

—Thirty per cent is a lot.

—And in the same paper on the same day we read the headline: SWISS INDUSTRY CONTINUES TO PROSPER. Good news, if you don't read the medical page.

The Old Man lays down the newspaper and yawns.

—Grandfather, you're tired.

—What were we talking about?

—About our army.

The Old Man has to yawn again: I'm talking about the army that carries out manoeuvres on our territory, the army of Swiss finance and its officer class; and you're talking about our army—*

The Grandson takes the poker: Now it's smoking again!

—The question is simply how is Switzerland to be defended, and then there's the fact that we don't all mean the same Switzerland . . . You know what I would like to see in place of the next great military review, Jonas: a week of citizens in uniform. A week all over the country when all Swiss citizens fit for service turn up at their workplaces in military uniforms. Nothing more. What do you think of it? The whole thing without the military rituals. Everything as usual. The editor of this newspaper will be sitting in his office as usual, but when he issues commands to his sub-editors or his correspondents, he will do so as a colonel—

The Grandson stands up: I'll fetch some more wood,

---

* Of course it is also the Army of the NCOs' clubs, innkeepers and their regular customers in certain regions and of those who take part in full-kit runs (sport as the Fatherland or *vice versa*) and of many mothers; indeed, it's not so simple.

Grandfather.

The Grandson goes down to the cellar.

—And after a week I'll call you up and you can tell me what has struck you. Can you hear me? To what extent the cadres in business and industry and the press are identical with our military cadres, and then we'll consider whose bodyguard this army is . . .

The Grandson comes back with a pile of wood.

—Thanks, Jonas, thanks.

—Birch, chestnut. What's this?

—Elder, perhaps.

The Grandson places a large branch in the fireplace.

—What was I trying to say, Jonas?

—I don't know.

—They're not afraid of war. Believe me! They haven't the courage to feel afraid. They're simply worried about their power. And yet they hold all the reins in their hands. A club for paranoiacs. Do you know why this Switzerland always feels threatened? Wherever I listen I hear their fear of being seen through, wherever I look I see excessive wealth . . . What I meant to say was—

The Grandson looks at his wrist-watch.

—If I were your age, Jonas, I'd emigrate.

The Old Man sees the empty bottle: Shall we have another Jeninser?

—I have to go, Grandfather.

The Old Man puts the empty bottle away: Why should we do away with the army?

—Why shouldn't we do away with it?

—It won't let itself be done away with, Jonas.

—Then what's the point of this referendum?

—It reinforces our feeling that what the army is defending is a democracy . . . Jonas, just think what holds our dear Switzerland together. The Francophones and Zürich, the Ticinese and Bern, to say nothing of the Juras. A Swiss Federal Railway, no matter how reliable, and the postage stamps common to all regions, don't constitute a nation. And prosperity obviously doesn't either. You can get rich as a German or an

American or whatever too. We have a flag, sure, and you see it everywhere—on inns and at barracks and on steamers on Sunday and during gymnastic competitions and at the Olympics among many other flags. Sure. But there's not a lot of faith floating around this flag. At most, we're a skiing nation. In winter.

—So what does hold Switzerland together?

—Precisely the army, as folklore.

The Grandson empties his glass and says nothing.

—Am I talking too much again?

The Grandson looks into his empty glass: The army as folklore!

The Grandson takes the glasses into the kitchen.

—Jonas, what do you have against folklore?

—What do you mean by folklore? The carnival in Basel, the Grisons with their March Calanda or whatever it's called, Zürich and its Six Bells . . .*

—But is a man from Geneva at home at the Basel Carnival? What does the Zürich Six Bells mean to someone from Ticino? By contrast, the army as folklore is shared by all.

—So there can be no Switzerland without the army!

—The army as folklore. And in case the great financial crash occurs. Worldwide. That's happened once this century. Who is going to pay the creditors? The unemployed and the tenants who'll be out in the street and the pensioners who'll stay at home? Or Big Brother: the Swiss banks? The army will show

---

* A spring festival with a procession: wigs and three-cornered hats and crinolines in a nostalgic recreation of the corporate state prior to Napoleon. An ophthalmologist or an advertising consultant who wants to be one of the gang can ride with the guild of carpenters; a senior manager can march with the guild of butchers; a professor is happy to wear the clean leather apron of the guild of coopers, which is followed by the guild of camel-drivers (not on camels, but in Arab dress); I recognize a councillor who is just having trouble with his horse and a public prosecutor, sweating with the guild of saffron-makers, who is throwing bouquets on to the pavement when the snowman Böög is burnt on the stroke of six watched by the public on foot, many holding a hot sausage and rejoicing over the Good Old Times . . .

who's boss. As it did in 1918. *

—Grandfather, those are memories of the past!

A pause.

—Jonas, what is it you want to be convinced of?

A clock in the village strikes the hour. Silence. Then it strikes the same hour again.

—You're right. The red mob with a clenched fist is a thing of the past. The bored crowds that throng the arcades in Locarno are thoroughly well-dressed. What they are staring into the windows for God knows! They've already got everything. And just like in the windows: *á la mode*. But they have to stand and stare at everything on sale. It's a compulsion. People who will never surf or dive have to look at the equipment and check out the prices. After that they stand in front of a window full of watches, which they've already got, or gold jewellery. The fact is they've already eaten. Their wretchedness lies in having purchasing power without any Great Hope, being stupefied by products. They spend their holidays in the service of our economic growth.

The Grandson says nothing.

—Are you going already?

—If the situation were the way you see it, if our army is actually a swindle, why don't you come out and say it. According to you the army is meant to be used only for domestic purposes, right?

---

* There was poverty. The rising inflation and the economic misery of the dependents of the armed forces personnel, who received no compensation for the cessation of wages, forced the authorities to provide cheap food: emergency meals in a gymnasium. As a seven-year-old I didn't notice much. My father, an unemployed architect, tried his hand as a small-scale broker. My mother, who as the daughter of an established family from Basel, felt terribly ashamed of what she was doing when she acted as look-out as I climbed fences to steal windfalls. I remember apple purées without sugar or, for a change, apples baked on the living-room stove, when there were once more no coins for the gas. I enjoyed collecting acorns in the forest more than the acorn coffee. My elder brother (weak after a severe attack of flu) got Ovaltine; I felt guilty when I pinched some of it. Our father was opposed to the red mob that went out on to the streets, indeed, even on to the parade ground in Zürich, unarmed. Even afterwards no arms câche could be found to substantiate the suspicion that there were plans for a violent revolution.

—Which is part of total defence.

—That's rubbish, Grandfather, excuse me.

—I'm listening.

—For a bodyguard for the bourgeoisie, as you see it, lightly armed tanks, automatic weapons, perhaps trench mortars, would be sufficient, a few dozen of those Pilatus planes Pinochet tried out on his own citizens, and helicopters, yes, definitely helicopters—

—And crews that obey orders.

—I mean—

—Jonas, do you know the oath of allegiance?

—I mean, as a bodyguard for the bourgeoisie the Swiss army is seriously over-equipped, Grandfather, you must admit that.

—I admit that.

—What are all the heavy Leopard tanks for, and the new US interception planes that cost billions and billions? What's all this high technology equipment for?

—A good question.

—What for?

—They don't want anyone in the country to notice what this Swiss army is really there for. The people could never be talked into accepting a federal security police. You've got to have a high-technology army, otherwise people will recognize it as a federal security police force.

A pause.

—Shall we put another log on the fire, Grandfather?

You're laughing . . .

—You and your Switzerland!

The Grandson laughs and stretches: I'm interested in information technology.

—You think everything else is out of date—

—I'm not an ex-serviceman, you know.

—I hope you never will be, Jonas.

—I'm interested in information technology.

The Grandson stretches again.

—Your generation thinks globally. Is that what you mean? Information technology is global. Switzerland without the army or the army without Switzerland, what do you care! And yet you keep saying: our army.

—That's what it's called . . .

The Grandson pushes a log into the fireplace.

—Jonas, what riles you?

—Patriotism.

—Whose patriotism?

—Yours, Grandfather.

A pause.

—You and your Switzerland . . .

A pause.

—Jonas, it's smoking.

The Grandson picks up the poker.

—I find your suspicion exaggerated. Perhaps our top brass are really convinced that their army could protect the population if it is sufficiently well armed.

—I'm sure they are.

—After all, they are military experts.

—And managing directors.

—Why should they lie to themselves?

—Their hats look good in a cloakroom, like those in the Hotel Adler; there's always something touching about those tall, empty hats trimmed with gold, I admit.

The Grandson hangs up the poker: What is it you find touching?

—The battles of Morgarten and Sempach. Yes, as a boy I used to collect them, dozens of little pictures of the battles to fill an album. It was a chocolate promotion, I think—I was crazy about them. Morgarten and Sempach and St Jakob-on-the-Birs, but that was a long time ago, so was Marignano. Is that enough to enable an army to understand itself today? We haven't even suffered a defeat—like the Polish army, the Dutch army, the French army, the Russian army, yes, even Hitler's army and the Italian army, the Japanese army—I can somehow understand that our officer class is extremely sensitive when their army is not treated as a legend.

The Grandson coughs and opens the window.

—Don't catch cold, Jonas!

The Old Man continues: It may be that, without our watch on the Mutschellen, the *Wehrmacht* would have simply gone through. In one night. It wouldn't have needed a week as in Holland and

Belgium . . . Or maybe Hitler thought to himself that once Swiss industry was in German hands it would have been bombed like the Rühr; our industry was able to deliver the goods more reliably if he left the Swiss army in peace. Neutrality often brings advantages to others. And we should immediately have blown up the Gotthard—I'm not kidding, Jonas. Your Grandfather, and that's me, personally packed the Devil's Bridge in the Schöllenen Gorge with dynamite. With his own hands. Did you ever notice those chambers in the piers, high up above the seething waters of the Reuss, and the narrow ladder leading up to them? Yes?

—No.

—Old soldiers' tales.

The Old Man makes a dismissive gesture.

—Jonas, why do we bother thinking!

The Old Man stands up and laughs: Just like in the picture album, yes, that's how it was. When we were guarding the St Gotthard stretch by Amsteg, where there's a small power station, or in Ticino: with rifles in our hands in spite of the blizzard. Like in the album for the Swiss family. It really was like that. Some of us did wonder what was in the long goods-trains on their way to Italy, one after the other, especially by night. Rühr coal? We didn't wonder too deeply. Switzerland was dependent on the good will of the Axis powers, who needed our St Gotthard Pass. When the invasion of Sicily had finally been launched, we did think: maybe there is military equipment in the long goods-trains. The Germans were defending themselves down there. Monte Cassino! Sometimes there may have been German troops too, whose nocturnal trips south we were watching over, rifle in hand—and when a chestnut fell with a thud, the safety catch was off in a flash: Halt, who goes there!—in keeping with our armed neutrality.

The Old Man closes the window: It's getting cool.

He sits down by the fireside again: Now let's make ourselves cosy . . .

The fire crackles.

—So you're studying information technology?

—I told you that just now, Grandfather. I hope it works out. I'd like to go to California for a couple of semesters, you know—

The telephone rings.

—Aren't you going to answer it, Grandfather?

—No.

—Shall I answer it?

—No.

The telephone goes on ringing.

—Is it someone who is going to abuse you again?

—It will stop eventually . . .

The telephone goes on ringing.

—Jonas, what is information technology?

The Grandson picks up the telephone: Hello . . . Hello! . . . Hello—

The Grandson puts down the receiver, the Old Man yawns: Now let's make ourselves cosy!

The fire crackles.

A pause.

—Why are you standing up? Why don't you sit by the fireside? Even if we don't drink any more Jeninser.

The Grandson sits down: Do you mind if I smoke?

—You never thought of being a conscientious objector, Grandfather?

—No.

—Would you advise anyone to do so?

—If you're motivated by religious conscience, Jonas, you don't need any advice. And it makes no difference to you to know that it's left to a military court to decide what conscience is. *

---

* I have experienced four or five drumhead services. Generally the wooden Protestant pulpit stands at the edge of a wood or in a clearing or among pear trees, never in the barrack-square or by the armoury; somewhere countrified, if possible with a view of the Alps, appropriate to God 'who gave us this beautiful land.' A treeless alp with an abandoned dairy-farm is ideal. When the chaplain comes in sight: BATTERY ATTEN-SHUN! And with this our captain, who so rarely wears his helmet, hands his battery over to the chaplain, who, a captain himself, salutes unsmartly with his right hand to his cap; a pocket Bible in the other hand. BATTERY AT EASE! And the sergeant-major adds: HELMETS OFF! which also applies to officers. And this makes a difference: a row of heads with hair and no badges of rank. The sermon is timeless (taken over from Warsaw-Oradour-Dunkirk-Lidice-Coventry-

—Ethics are not tied to religion.

—The alternative would be conscientious objection on political grounds, which can't be countenanced. You know that. That would get the constitutional state into trouble. So it would be prison, Jonas.

—You get fourteen months now!

—And what would you achieve politically?

—I know someone it destroyed.

—What do you mean?

—Platzspitz Park and so on. *

—What is political consciousness anyway? There are lots of

Leningrad-Dresden etc) and by no means too long, compared with the time we spend drilling. It is permissible to fold one's hands in reverence, but not mandatory. Do I believe in God and in particular in Jesus as the Son of God? As a gunner I can utter the Amen or not. HELMETS ON! Or else we sing: 'Fatherland, you may rest secure.' Not everyone can sing but everyone has to try, and that's what it sounds like. BATTERY ATTEN-SHUN! Thereupon the chaplain puts his cap back on and leaves the pulpit. What did the chaplain say to us? It was always the same: loyalty to the army equals loyalty to God!—as in every army on this earth.

* This is the name of the public park, behind the Swiss National Museum, away from busy Zürich with its shop windows, where the wretched world of the drug addicts is played out. Last summer I visited the melancholy spot with a friend. An attempt to get into conversation with an addict, whose whole forearm was covered by a bandage, didn't get very far; his arm was agonizing, he said, but suddenly he looked away and pretended to be deaf. He scented plain-clothes police. Then he said simply: No one helps us. In the pavilion, where they had already set up their beds of rags for the night, I managed to have a long conversation with a man who obviously had no dope: he was standing. Did he have friends here? He laughed drily; he certainly didn't have any anywhere else. He was thirty-one. What did he hope for? Another damn fool question! We both leaned against the balustrade. An elegant little pavilion for a Sunday morning concert under the old plane trees. Those sitting on the ground already had a candle in front of them. Hope? His answer came like a delayed echo: None. What was I doing here? He obviously thinks me too old for a plain-clothes policeman. I'm a writer. That seems to annoy him; we're still leaning on the decorative balustrade, but he says no more. When I say goodbye and leave, he doesn't nod in reply. Elsewhere an ambulance drives by, with a blue light, but it causes no excitement in the park. That happens here. On the broad steps leading up to the National Museum, a

people who wouldn't need one if a PR firm didn't urge them to
acquire it. And then it's not a political consciousness of your
own, Jonas, that develops from within you and that develops you
. . . Now I'm talking like a grandfather. Yes.
   —If only there was community service—
The Grandson remains silent, without looking at the Old Man.
   —What are you brooding over, Jonas?
   —Arse-licking!
   —Please don't shout.
   —Arse-licking!
   —That's the school of life.
   —So they say!
   —Yes, Jonas, you'd better learn on the barrack-square what
lies ahead of you. The school of life—there's something to that.
The time comes to get away from Mummy! It's hard to imagine
how much arse-licking has gone on at the state's expense in little
Switzerland alone, and it gets some people further than others,
some as far as the Federal Parliament.
   —You think there's any other kind of society?
   —Just think of the east-bloc States!
   A pause.
   —I have a friend, Grandfather, a doctor, older than me,
who's in prison right now. Because he doesn't believe in civil
defence. In prison in a manner of speaking. During the day he
can go to his work in the hospital, only he spends his free
evenings and the night in the local gaol, and of course weekends.

---

young person is lying, obviously female, wearing white trousers. I
overcome my inhibition about being a voyeur and see that the artificial
respiration is already in progress. Two ambulance men on their knees. A
drug addict is haranguing those standing around in a circle: You don't
even know the emergency number and just leave someone lying there! The
artificial respiration is having no effect. My companion whispers to me,
'This is serious Doctor, she's had it!' When one of her friends comes along,
a fellow who pushes the bystanders out of the way and shouts:
'Erika!'—she comes to. 'Get up, Erika,' he shouts, 'Get up!' And she
manages to sit up, as the man tugs on her belt: 'Come on, Erika, get up!'
A pretty young woman with a lot of black hair, she opens her big black
eyes like the cow eyes of Pallas Athene, for a few seconds, then she
collapses again and no amount of cursing, cajoling or shaking is any use.

—And now Easter is coming, that's bad luck.

—He has a family.

—Why did you mention this?

—He refuses to take part in civil defence, while the army holds radiated territory. As a doctor, he won't have anything to do with it, he says. It was his third refusal; up to now they had tried fines because fines don't attract publicity. Have you heard of this International Association of Physicians or whatever it's called?

—In New York, yes.

—Civil defence, he says, amounts to criminal deception on the part of the government, and he was able to prove this in court.

—International Physicians For The Prevention Of Nuclear War, that's the exact name of the organization—I know one of the American scientists personally; he visited Hiroshima and wrote about it, Robert Lifton.

—And then if you take a look at what our Federal Department of Civil Defence has to offer in its publications . . . You know, a picture of a Swiss soldier with a helmet and an assault rifle pointed at the enemy, confident that his loved ones are safely tucked away in an air-raid shelter. Probably the old people are playing cards and the children Monopoly, until months or years later, as they were promised, the All Clear sounds and they come out into the daylight—there's an illustration of this!—and presumably go off to the supermarket to buy fresh yoghurt. Have you ever seen these publications?

—Jonas, you're laughing—

—The farmer brushes down his cow to get rid of the radioactivity; the Mother goes out with the garden hose to make sure the lettuce isn't dangerous; the soldier comes home and the construction industry rebuilds Switzerland.

—Jonas, who reads a book like that?

—What's your opinion, Grandfather?

—Jonas . . .

—Are you tired, Grandfather?

—Must one always have an opinion!

—My last question. What's your opinion about our civil defence?

—Jonas . . .

117

—Grandfather, I shan't say it again.

—That's something I wouldn't tell any grandson.

—OK.

The Old Man picks up a pipe.

—I thought you'd given up smoking, Grandfather.

—That's why I don't have any tobacco.

—Grandfather, how old are you?

—Gorbachev has realized that there's not much alternative left for the Russians. Bankruptcy through over-production of arms or common sense. They're not disarming out of love for us. That may make things difficult for Switzerland as an army. Our experts have sensed that. An army without a fixed enemy gets edgy. When you're on manoeuvres and the announcement comes: Enemy attacking, I'm sure no one thinks of Eskimos—

—No.

—You're laughing, Jonas, but the more sensible the Russians get—the Soviet Union, I mean—the more urgent becomes the search for an internal enemy. And it's getting serious. No one will admit what this Swiss army is really there for.

The Grandson stands and picks up his leather jacket.

—General Rogers, an expert, I should say, a NATO General and an American—General Rogers has written that a war in Europe cannot remain conventional; he reckons three or four days, which would be time enough to settle into our civilian shelters, and you know the scientific prognosis, you mentioned it: the deadly radiation won't stop at our borders, as Chernobyl has taught us, and that was merely a minor melt-down. Jonas, what are our Leopard tanks in the Toggenburg and the thirty-four American interception planes in the air supposed to do while the population is dying of radiation sickness?

The Grandson puts on his leather jacket.

—Without our faith in shelters, Jonas, the Swiss army makes no sense, or at least not the sense they tell us about.

—That's logical.

—And for that reason the civil defence force is also to be armed, I hear. Anyone who, when the crisis comes, doesn't go into the shelters but prefers to meet his end in his library or looking up at the Mythen Mountains is to be treated as a deserter, as the internal enemy: he may believe in life after death but not in all seven federal councillors combined.

The Grandson looks at the Old Man: There are times, Grandfather, when I don't know if you are speaking seriously or if you think you're making a joke . . .

—Seriously, Jonas. Seriously: getting rid of the army would mean the birth of a different Switzerland. Just imagine, a living, forward-looking Switzerland. That's what people are afraid of. And to prevent that—

—We need the army.

—Exactly.

The Old Man counts on his fingers: We need the army, *first*, as the school of life.

—Arse-licking . . .

—Second?

—*Second*, as the school for men.

The Grandson buttons his leather jacket.

—Your dear Papa never taught you to stand to attention when you're spoken to. And where else could you learn to give orders? I don't believe you can even play the corporal with your younger sisters, not even with your mother. To take responsibility, Jonas—that's something you learn in the army more cheaply than anywhere else.[*] If the orders you give are nonsense, the troops can grumble to themselves—as an officer that costs you nothing. In the crisis even grumbling won't help. And if the troops annoy you: punishment drill! A sergeant-major takes care of that . . .

---

[*] There was something like jubilation in Malvaglia, where for months we had been practising *left turn—right turn—forward march*, when one morning the order of the day read: 0900 hours, race for officers, non-commissioned officers and men in gym-shorts and gym-shoes. The course ran from Malvaglia via Motto, Ludiano and Semione almost as far as Biasca and back to Malvaglia, an estimated ten kilometres. That's to say, no marathon. At the double, of course, and we'd show the sergeant-major. And it was always something of a pleasure to see our officers in gym-shorts. So we were looking forward to the race. Then suddenly a higher authority, probably Divisional Command, issued different orders: 0900-1000 hours tetanus injections. Our captain had to acquiesce. So we got our injections. I had nothing

Last time I saw you you told me about your girl-friend.
—What makes you think of that?
—Didn't she run off?
—Does that bother you?
—An army unit, even a small defence unit, can't run off and leave you, Jonas, and you can give order after order until giving orders gets into your flesh and blood. Yes, and you can reply to one of those half-page ads: engineer wanted to fill a leading position.
The Grandson laughs half-heartedly.
—Jonas, we can't manage without any army!
—Thirdly?
—Commerce and industry don't only need experts who are paid for their obedience, but leaders, Jonas, personalities.
—Thirdly?
—Can you see that?
—More or less.
—*Thirdly*: as the school of the nation.
—Meaning?
—Don't you know that, Jonas?
—So we can't do without an army . . .
—Without helmets and without camouflage dress, how could we make a nation out of an international financial centre even if it *is* beginning to stink to high heaven? How could we do it, hand on your heart? Or do you think a shared interest in protecting the environment would be enough? Where would you learn love of your homeland, Jonas, if not from your superior officers?

---

against inoculation; some men wanted to refuse, but orders are orders. The smell of this serum is repulsive; the thin incision almost imperceptible. I fainted in the village square. A sudden vertigo, but there was no need for a stretcher. The medical team took me down to the nearest battery or company in the valley. The order came: all troops are to rest for two hours. Then came the start of the ten-kilometre race. Our medical corporal called it madness. Tell the captain! He reported to the battery office, where our captain was smoking cigarillos non-stop: as a medical student (in about his tenth semester) he had doubts about a race following a tetanus inoculation. But the race was on the order of the day . . . Three or four, including a first lieutenant, passed out on the course, but at no cost to military insurance.

—Fourthly?

—*Fourthly*: as a bodyguard for our plutocracy. *

—That's an obsession with you, Grandfather.

—*Fifthly*—

—What do they need a bodyguard for?

—To feel secure, I imagine.

—You think the people are planning a revolution?

—Don't say the people, please! What we have in our country is a *population*. And a population never plans revolution; on the contrary, it's afraid of revolution—and how!—and this fear is used to lead it by the nose.

—So who is going to start a revolution?

—Ask the gentlemen of the General Staff.

—A revolution by lefties like you, Grandfather?

The Grandson laughs heartily.

—When our middle class entered history, they were men with minds of their own, Jonas, and they meant what they said about democracy. But a hundred years of rule—that's always a bit too long . . .

—Grandfather, what are you trying to say?

—After wearing out their own values, it's natural that this middle class should hide behind thick walls. Entirely natural. DEFEND THE BEGINNINGS! That was 1968, Jonas, when you were still dribbling in your play-pen. I know people who were maltreated by the Zürich police at that time, a young woman who had nothing whatever to do with the demonstration; she happened to get in the way of the water-cannon, fell down and was dragged off to the Globus cellar. There she was kicked in the belly by an unidentified policeman . . . And they succeeded. They established law and order and a society characterized primarily by economic growth, with a profit mania, a sickness.

—Fifthly?

---

* For example: 0.5 per cent of the population owns fifty per cent of the taxable wealth. That's to say, out of 200 Swiss one Swiss owns as much as the other 199 together. As to real estate: out of ten Swiss one owns eighty per cent of the real estate. I picture ten Swiss standing in front of ten chairs and it turns out that eight of these chairs are not free but belong to one single Swiss. But he rents out.

—Their reassurance is the army.

—Fifthly?

—*Fifthly*; how would we Swiss look to ourselves, Jonas, without a military display from time to time? Without a fly-past once a week, zooming over the valley and zooming back again. I always look up and say to myself: That's us. Everyone else has stuff like that too, sure, but so do we.

The Grandson is looking for something.

—I'm looking for my scarf.

—I hung it up outside.

—How are you going to vote in the referendum then, Grandfather?

—I no longer go to the ballot-box, you know. Going to the ballot-box makes me one of the vanishing minority.

—And if you don't go to the ballot-box?

—Then I'm one of the majority.

—But it's important, Grandfather. It's not just a question of putting a question-mark in front of their army, it's a demand for a comprehensive peace policy.*

---

* A question: when we talk about peace, and assuming we believe in the possibility of peace, how do we imagine it? In 1946 in Frankfurt-am-Main, as the guest of bombed-out Germans, I understood by peace quite simply: no more bombs, no more victories, the release of prisoners of war. In Prague, almost free of bomb damage, after a visit to Theresienstadt, where I still saw the gallows and thousands of bags containing human ashes, the answer also seemed simple: peace as the end of fear, no uniforms of foreign domination. In Warsaw, in 1948, after walking for hours through the silence of the ruins, I suddenly heard the thud of riveters at work on the first pylon of a new bridge over the Vistula: peace! There, the conversation (accompanied by half-cigarettes) with contemporaries was about the only thing they still possessed: the great hope that from the ruins will arise the new man. One lot were awaiting him as Communists, the others as Christians. Now we know that the new man has not appeared. Our sensible rejection of war as a means of politics does not imply that we are yet capable of peace. Societies with power structures may wish for non-war, peace would contradict their essential nature. Since no ruling class will ever admit that it needs an army to use, under certain circumstances, against its own population, it is compelled to

—I'm gradually getting to know our country.

—What do you mean by that?

—A peace policy? A Swiss peace policy?

—Does someone want war here?

—War here, no.*

—War somewhere else?

—No, but profit wherever and whenever possible.

The Grandson picks up an apple and bites into it.

—I was in a luxury clinic when one of our countrymen spoke to me. He asked what I thought about joining the UN. I told him I don't like talking in the sauna. Joining the UN won't gain us anything, he said. And that's what most of the Swiss think. Strongly. That we might contribute something ourselves is an un-Swiss idea, Jonas.

The Grandson bites into the apple.

—Do you really want to drive now?

—Sure.

—But it's raining. You're on a motorbike.

The Grandson opens the door and steps out: —There's a

conceal this function of the army behind a form of rearmament that promises defence against the whole world. A society capable of peace would be a society that got along without images of an enemy. Prosperity alone does not guarantee this possibility . . . I don't know whether the species' will to survive will be powerful enough to enable human society to change to the point of being capable of peace. Let us hope so. The matter is urgent. Praying for peace does not absolve us from facing the question of what to do with this hope, which is a radical one. Faith in the possibility of peace (and hence in humanity's survival) is a revolutionary faith.

*The Grandfather has obviously forgotten that as a grammar school pupil I reported to the FMV (Voluntary Pre-military Training), whereupon I received a beret with a cockade, a belt with cartridge pockets, a long rifle and a jacket from the armoury. I wanted to become a man. There is something enjoyable about the military rituals of subordination, no doubt about it. So we spent our Saturday afternoons doing obstacle runs and drill as well as shooting with live ammunition and singing on the march, led by a genuine lieutenant. His name was Züblin and he later became a renowned corps commander. I used to feel uncomfortable carrying my long rifle in the street-car, although no one ever asked me what it was for. And after a year I left. For no specific reason.

clear sky, almost a clear sky.

The clock in the village strikes twelve.

—We've been chatting all this time . . .

The Grandson closes the door: —Take care, Grandfather.

—Karin comes back tomorrow.

The clock in the village strikes again.

—That's the way it goes here: our church clock strikes twice. When people have been in the fields or in the forest, it suddenly booms through the valley. Yes, but did you count right? So after a while it strikes again so that you can check, to make sure: ten, eleven, twelve. Really.

The Grandson fetches his crash helmet: Why didn't you emigrate, Grandfather?

—I often wonder.

The Grandson shakes hands.

—*Ciao!*

—Drive carefully.

The Grandson leaves.

—Don't forget your scarf!

The Old Man stands up and looks to see if the bottle is really empty. The engine can be heard starting. The Old Man takes the blue paperback out of the bookcase again and turns to the last page; the sound of the engine fades; the Old Man stands and reads out with the voice of a schoolboy compelled to read aloud something he has difficulty understanding:

> I didn't dare to think what is unthinkable. Obedience out of apathy, but also obedience out of belief in the Confederation hallowed by an oath. As a gunner, I didn't want to fire my gun without faith, if war started. I didn't want to know but to believe. That's how it was, I believe.

He tosses the little book into the fireplace.

—Yes, we're pretty cowardly, Jonas . . .

The Old Man switches out the light.

Translated from the German by Michael Bullock.

FRIEDRICH
DÜRRENMATT
VÁCLAV HAVEL
IN ZÜRICH

Friedrich Dürrenmatt

D ear Václav Havel:
    In 1968, in the Stadtheater in Basel, there was a
    protest meeting against the invasion of Czechoslovakia.
I was there and I spoke, and I closed my address with these
words:

> In Czechoslovakia, human liberty has lost one battle in
> the struggle for a fairer world, but not the war: the war
> will continue against violent ideologues everywhere,
> whether they be wearing the mask of communism, ultra-
> communism or democracy. The Czechoslovak people
> have given us an example of how to conduct such a
> struggle in a developed country without a jungle to
> disappear into: in order to avoid a massacre, the
> Czechoslovak people have declined to use their own
> army, but their non-violent resistance has dealt a blow
> to a great superpower that may be more grievous than
> we can presently imagine.

More than twenty years have passed. The United States has
lost a war and its honour, in Vietnam. The power of the hard-
liners in Eastern Europe has crumbled away, and the bristling
military blocks on both sides have lost their function: the clichéd
pictures of the enemy have lost all relevance, as each superpower
is increasingly confronted not by the other, but by its own
internal problems. And non-violent resistance has found an
ambassador in you, dear Havel, and Czechoslovakia a president.
    You have just received the Gottlieb Duttweiler Prize. The
prize is named after a popular but controversial figure in
Switzerland, a man who transformed his own large business into
a co-operative and who founded one of the few political parties
in this country that can still be called oppositional.
    We are told, dear Havel, that you were awarded this prize
because your name is synonymous with principle, honesty and
tolerance of others' views: three pillars of individual freedom in a
democratic society. It's a fine prize, a Swiss prize, but I
sometimes wish it could be the other way round. I can't imagine
you awarding a Václav Havel Prize to a Swiss conscientious
objector for his principles or his honesty or—but wait: how can it

ever be said that you, of all people, were tolerant? I don't get this: how tolerant were you of the regime in Czechoslovakia? True, you refused to go abroad—that was a kind of tolerance: you accepted your punishment and went to prison. And, by so doing, you brought about the collapse of a regime. In contrast, there are our conscientious objectors . . . It so happens that the Swiss are a warlike people, even though no one has attacked us for over two hundred years. But we are ready for them when they come. And just to prove it we insist that every Swiss citizen be ready to defend Switzerland, and we lock up anyone honest or principled enough to say that they cannot do it. If the character of the objection is religious, that provides grounds for leniency, but if it is political—as was the case with you, dear Havel—then the whole severity of the law falls upon the objector, as happened to you in Czechoslovakia. Our conscientious objectors are our dissidents. So far they haven't achieved anything.

I don't want to bang on about great Swiss victories—the Hussite Wars that shook the whole of Europe, or the defeat of King Ottokar II of Bohemia by Aargauer Rudolf von Habsburg with his Switzers, or the Habsburgs themselves, a dynasty of Swiss émigrés, against whose return home the Swiss fought successfully—but it was precisely the collapse of the old Swiss Confederation in 1798 that led to the creation of the new one, that led to modern Switzerland. Similarly modern Czechoslovakia came into being with the end of World War One in 1918. Both states were created by defeat. In the case of the Swiss, it was our own defeat; in the case of Czechoslovakia it was the defeat of Austria–Hungary. And then Hitler came along. When the great powers left Czechoslovakia in the lurch in 1938 there was a thanksgiving service in the cathedral in Bern. Czechoslovakia put up no fight then, and the Sudetenland was annexed, and soon afterwards the Czech provinces were made a Protectorate, and then Slovakia became a vassal state. I wonder if Switzerland

---

Overleaf: Karl Schnyder, City President, in his office. Alfred Sarasin of A. Sarasin & CIE, banker. Photographs by Alex Kayser.

would have defended itself in that situation. It remains a hypothetical question; the situation never arose. But for the Czechs, it was a catastrophe. Think of Lidice—they were made to work for Hitler, and the Jews were gassed. We were not attacked, but we also had to work for Hitler, and the Jews, whom we turned back at our frontiers, were also gassed.

After the war, Czechoslovakia fell victim to Stalin, and to the politics of his successors. The attempt to reform communism and give it a human face was put down by force, as it had been previously in the German Democratic Republic and in Hungary. You, Václav Havel, described it all in your essay, 'Event and Totality':

> In the fifties, there were enormous concentration camps in our country, in which tens of thousands of innocent people were detained. In the same period the 'New Faith' had tens of thousands of believers who thronged the building-sites and sang communist anthems. Executions and torture, dramatic flights across the borders, conspiracies co-existed with poems written in praise of the Dictator in Chief. The President of the Republic signed the death warrants of his closest friends but, strangely, it was also possible to run into him on the street from time to time. The singing of fanatical idealists, the rantings of evil politicians and the suffering of heroes have been part of history for as long as we can remember. The fifties were a bad time, but there have been many such in history. One could classify them with other, similar periods, or at least offer comparisons; they still somehow have the impression of being history. No one would say that nothing had happened in this period, that it was uneventful. The crucial document of the regime that was installed after the Soviet invasion of 1968 was called *The Lessons of the Crisis Years*. It was an accurate title: the regime really did learn its lessons. It saw that opening the door just a hand's breadth to acknowledge other views and interests would imperil its own existence. So from then on, it concentrated

exclusively on self-preservation: the means of directly and indirectly manipulating the lives of its citizens were taken to new lengths, acquired a dynamism of their own; nothing could be left the chance any longer. The last nineteen years in Czechoslovakia are almost a textbook example of a mature totalitarian system: revolutionary ethos and terror replaced by dogged immobility, neurotic caution, bureaucratic anonymity, a mindless stereotype bent only on perfecting itself. The singing of the enthusiast and the wailing of the tortured are no longer heard; arbitrary rule has put on silk gloves and left the torture-chambers for the plush offices of the bureaucrats. The only time you get to see the president nowadays is behind the bullet-proof glass of his limousine, as he races to the airport, surrounded by his police escort, to welcome Colonel Gadhaffi. This mature totalitarian system has such sophisticated, complex and powerful instruments of manipulation at its command, that it no longer needs its killers and its victims. And still less does it need enthusiastic builders of Utopia; their dreams of a better future only make for disorder. This era's tag for itself, 'really existing socialism,' tells you what it has no use for: dreamers.

In contrast, Václav Havel, by now president yourself, when you expounded in your New Year address of 1990 the society that these 'dreamers' had in mind, you described a republic 'that is independent, free, democratic, economically flourishing but also socially just, a human republic in short, serving the citizen and hoping that the citizen will reciprocate and serve it. A republic of widely educated people, because without such people, none of our problems could be solved.'

Of the two societies you've described, it is this second one, this independent, free and democratic republic, that the Swiss dream of living in; they dream the same dream as you, Václav Havel. But the reality in which the Swiss dream is different.

Overleaf: Bernard Christ, lawyer, with his children.

131

As a playwright, you portrayed the world in which you used to live in plays which critics describe as absurd theatre. For me, these plays were not absurd or meaningless, but tragic grotesques: what is more grotesque than the topsy-turvy, paradoxical outcome of taking an intrinsically reasonable idea like communism—is it possible to describe a more equitable social order?—and putting it into effect? Everything man touches, he turns upon its head; reason becomes unreason; justice injustice; freedom unfreedom.

It is possible to see Switzerland as a grotesque like your tragic grotesques: as a prison—admittedly different from the prisons you were thrown into—in which the Swiss have taken refuge. Because everything outside is wild and lawless, the Swiss feel safe from attack in their prison; they feel free, freer than other people. But they are prisoners of their neutrality.

The prison has only one problem: it must prove that it is not a prison. Seen from the outside, a prison is always a prison: its inmates are prisoners, and prisoners are not free. Seen from the outside, only the warders are free. The Swiss solution was this: the prisoners introduced compulsory warder service for themselves. The Swiss thus have the good fortune of being both prisoner and warder.

This special prison obviously needs no walls, because it is the prisoners who are warders guarding themselves, and, as we know, warders are free men. As free men the warders do business with one another and with the outside world—quite a business! But because the warders are also prisoners, they occasionally suspect that they might be prisoners and not free men, so the prison administration has compiled dossiers on everyone it suspects of harbouring feelings of imprisonment and unfreedom. Because the prison administration suspects quite a number of people might have these feelings, it has, in fact, a whole dossier-mountain range. When the warders come to hear of the dossiers that have been kept on them they suddenly feel themselves to be prisoners and not free. This, of course, is exactly what the prison administration wants them *not* to feel. And so, in order to feel free again, the warders demand that the prison authorities tell them who started the dossiers. But the dossier-mountain range is so enormous that the prison administration can declare that it must have started by itself. Or rather, it was the fear of not being secure in the prison that gave rise to the mountain range of dossiers.

The fear is not unfounded. Who wouldn't want to be in a prison in which the prisoners are free? The prison becomes a world attraction; many people try to become prisoners, which they are permitted to do if they have the necessary means— freedom is a precious commodity—whereas those without the means are turned away.

Truly, the task of the prison administrators is unenviable. For instance there are not enough free prisoners to sweep and polish the luxury cells and the corridors so that the administrators have to admit people from outside, whom they then have to pay, just to keep the prison clean. These people are looked down upon as unfree by the other prisoners, who also earn money, but are free.

Although the prison appears to be flourishing, its business is so inextricably involved with other, outside businesses, that doubt arises about whether it really is a prison at all. Perhaps it has become merely an imaginary prison. To prove that the prison is real, the prison administrators—who have to justify their jobs—spend billions of francs arming the warders (who are their own prisoners) with modern weapons. Modern weapons eventually become obsolete and so they need to be replaced— regardless of the likelihood that war would mean the end of what they are trying to protect. In a disaster-prone technological world, the administrators are still indulging in their Nibelungen

---

Over the next six pages, in order: Nicolas Baer of the Bank Julius Baer. Hans R. Kuechler and Alfred R. Baumgartner, both of the Union Bank of Switzerland; Mr Kuechler oversees the arts sponsorship programme of the Union Bank of Switzerland. Claude de Saussure, of the bank Pictet & CIE, a descendant of Horace Benedict de Saussure, depicted on the Swiss twenty-franc note. The final photograph is of Mr de Saussure with his wife Marie Noelle outside their home, *Schloss vufflens*, owned by the de Saussure family since 1641.

de Saussure

Venti Franchi

strategy of absolute security, instead of realizing that they should be brave enough to abolish their warders and free their prisoners, even though Switzerland would then no longer be a prison, but a part of Europe.

The prison is losing its reputation. It is starting to have doubts. The administrators, always inclined to legislate their way out of difficulties insist that the prison is not in crisis, that the prisoners are free (the genuine prisoners, those loyal to the administration, anyway), whereas actually many prisoners believe that the prison is in crisis because the prisoners are not free. There is an internal debate in the prison, because the administration wants to celebrate the 700th anniversary of the alleged founding of the prison, even though it was at that time no prison at all, but rather a notorious nest of brigands. People aren't sure what they should celebrate, the prison or freedom. If the prison, the prisoners will feel imprisoned; a celebration of freedom will make the prison seem superfluous.

It was a peculiar feeling that came over me, my dear Havel, as I was writing this address. It is a feeling of embarrassment at the likelihood that you will be held up as proof to us that everything in our Western world is rosy, that there is nothing that beats freedom. We will, in all likelihood conveniently overlook what you wrote in your essay 'Attempt at Living in Truth':

> The traditional parliamentary democracies don't appear to offer any way of coping with a runaway technological civilization and a runaway industrial and consumer society. They find themselves in thrall to it and have no idea about how to deal with it. But their ways of manipulating people are infinitely finer and more sophisticated than the brutal methods of our post-totalitarian system. The whole stationary complex of rigid and unimaginative parties, acting only out of political necessity, controlled by professional party machines, and stripping the citizen of all concrete and personal responsibility, these complicated structures of

invisibly manipulative and invisibly expanding centres of capital accumulation, the all-pervading dictatorship of consumption, production, advertising, commerce, the consumer society, the excess of information, all this, so often analysed and described—it is almost impossible to see in it a perspective, a route by which man will find his way back to himself.

We should listen carefully to these sentences about our Western version of freedom, not least because they come from the ideological prison of 'really existing socialism'. Yes, we're proud of our direct democracy; yes, we have pensions for widows and orphans and for the old; we've surprised the world by giving the vote to women after all; and we're insured against death, illness, accident, burglary and fire: lucky fellow whose house burns down. Here in the West, politics has forsaken ideology for economics; its issues have become economic issues. Where should the state intervene and where not, whom should it support and whom not, whom should it tax, and what and how? Wages and working-hours are settled by negotiation. Peace is more of a threat to us than war. A harsh sentence, but not a cynical one. Our streets are battlefields; our atmosphere is filling with poison gases; our oceans are oil-puddles; our fields are contaminated by pesticides; the Third World is now being pillaged worse than the Holy Land once was by the Crusaders: no wonder it's trying to blackmail us now.

It isn't war that's the father of all things; it's peace. War springs from our failure to cope with peace. Peace is the problem we must solve. Peace has the deadly attribute of incorporating warfare. The driving force of the free market economy is competition, the struggle for markets, trade war. The free market economy puts the emphasis on freedom; perhaps the planned economy will stress justice. Perhaps the Marxist experiment was just ahead of its time. What can an individual do? You, Václav Havel, have asked, What now? The individual is an existential concept; economic systems, the state and its institutions are all collective concepts. Politics is to do with the collective, not the existential, but to be effective it has to appeal to the individual.

Man is more irrational than rational. He is governed more by his emotion than his understanding. Politics exploits that. Only thus can the parade of ideologies in our century be explained, appeals to good sense are unavailing, especially when a totalitarian ideology actually tries to look like sense. The individual must distinguish between what is feasible and what isn't. Society can never be just, free and fair, only more just, more free and more fair. What the individual has a right to insist on, what he must insist on, is what you insisted on, Václav Havel: human rights, enough to eat for everyone, equality before the law, freedom of expression, freedom of assembly, open government, the abolition of torture. All these are not utopian; they should be taken for granted as the birthright of man, as befitting human dignity. These are rights that don't ride roughshod over the individual, but govern his co-existence with other individuals. These are rights rights as an expression of tolerance—traffic regulations, so to speak. Human rights are existential rights, every new ideological revolution has tried to get rid of them, has called for a new type of man instead. It has been done so often. Václav Havel, your mission as President is the same as the mission of Václav Havel the dissident.

You are here among the Swiss, the Swiss have welcomed you, the Swiss President has received you, a former Swiss parliamentarian has delivered a eulogy to you, and I, a Swiss, have spoken as well, because we are fond of talking in Switzerland. What kind of people are we Swiss? To have been spared by fate is neither a disgrace nor a distinction, but it is a warning. Towards the end of his *Politicus*, Plato writes that after a man's death, his soul must choose a new life by lot: 'By chance, the soul of Odysseus received the very last lot of all, and now stepped up to make its choice. Remembering all its former travails, it had forsaken all ambition. It went around for a long time, looking for the life of a quiet, withdrawn man. At last it managed to find one, which the others had left unregarded. And finding it, it said it would have behaved no differently if it had received the very first lot, and that it chose its new life with joy.' I am convinced that Odysseus chose the lot of being Swiss.

JOHN BERGER
AND
JEAN MOHR
THE ZOO IN BASEL

*In memory of Peter Fuller and our many conversations
about the chain of being and neo-Darwinism.*

In Basel the zoo is almost next to the railway station. Most of
the larger birds in the zoo are free-flying, and so it can
happen that you see a stork or a cormorant flying home over
the marshalling yards. Equally unexpected is the ape house. It is
constructed like a circular theatre with three stages: one for the
gorillas, another for the orang-utans and a third for the
chimpanzees.

You take your place on one of the tiers—as in a Greek
theatre—or you can go to the very front of the pit and press your
forehead against the sound-proof plate glass. The lack of sound
makes the spectacle on the other side, in a certain way, sharper,
like mime. It also allows the apes to be less bothered by the
public. We are mute to them too.

All my life I have visited zoos, perhaps because going to the
zoo is one of my few happy childhood memories. My
father used to take me. We didn't talk much, but we
shared each other's pleasure and I was aware that his was largely
based on mine. Together we used to watch the apes, losing all
sense of time, each of us, in his fashion, pondering the mystery of
progeniture. My mother, on the rare occasions she came with us,
refused the higher primates. She preferred the newly discovered
pandas.

I tried to pull her towards the chimpanzees, but she would
reply—following her own logic: 'I'm a vegetarian and I only gave
it up, the practice not the principle, for the sake of you boys and
for Daddy.' Bears were another animal she liked. Apes, I can see
now, reminded her of the passions which lead to the spilling of
blood.

The audience in Basel is of all ages. From toddlers to
pensioners. No other spectacle in the world can attract
such a spectrum of the public. Some sit, like my father and
I once did, lost to the passing of time. Others drop in for a few
moments. There are *habitués* who come every day and whom the

actors recognize. But on nobody—not even the youngest toddler—is the dramatic evolutionary riddle lost: how is it that they are so like us and yet not us?

This is the question which dominates the dramas on each of the three stages. Today the gorillas' play is a social one about coming to terms with imprisonment: life sentences. On the second stage, the chimpanzees' show is cabaret: each performer has her or his own number. The orang-utans are performing *Werther* without words—soulful and dreamy. I am exaggerating? Of course, because I do not yet know how to define the real drama of the theatre in Basel.

Is any theatre possible without a conscious ritual of re-enactment? All theatre repeats, again and again, what once happened. Often those who are dead are brought back to life on the stage. Mere reflex actions do not make theatre; but wait—

Each stage has at least one private recess where an animal can go, if she or he wishes to leave the public, and from time to time they do so. Sometimes for quite long periods. When they come out to face the audience again, they are perhaps not so far from a practice of re-enactment. In the London zoo chimps pretend to eat and drink off invisible plates with non-existent glasses. A pantomime.

We can see that chimpanzees are as familiar as we are with fear. The Dutch zoologist Dr Kortlandt believes that in fact they have intimations of mortality. We are at least on the threshold of theatre.

In the first half of the century there were attempts to teach chimpanzees to talk—until it was discovered that the form of their vocal tract was unsuitable for the production of the necessary range of sounds. Later they were taught a deaf and dumb language, and a chimp called Washoe in Ellensburg near Seattle called a duck a water bird. Did this mean that Washoe had broken through a language barrier or had she just learned by rote? A heated debate followed (the distinction of man was at stake!) about what constitutes or doesn't a language for animals.

It was already known—thanks to the extraordinary work of Jane Goodall with her chimpanzees in Tanzania—that these

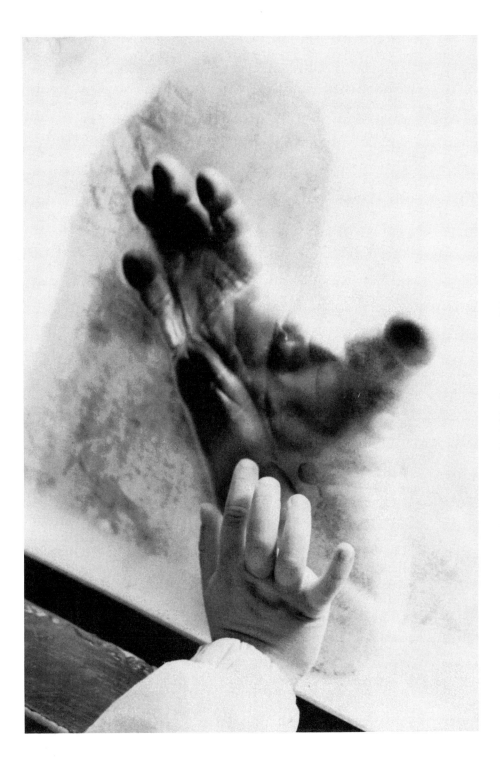

animals used tools, and that, language or no language, their ability to communicate with one another was both wide-ranging and subtle.

Another chimpanzee in the United States, named Sarah, underwent a series of tests conducted by Douglas Gillan, which were designed to show whether or not she could reason. Contrary to what Descartes believed, a verbal language may not be indispensable for the process of reasoning. Sarah was shown a video of her trainer playing the part of being locked in a cage and desperately trying to get out! After the film she was offered a series of pictures of varying objects to choose from. One, for instance, showed a lighted match. The picture she chose was of a key—the only object which would have been useful for the situation she had seen enacted on the video screen.

In Basel we are watching a strange theatre in which, on both sides of the glass, the performers may believe they are an audience. On both sides the drama begins with resemblance and the uneasy relationship that exists between resemblance and closeness.

The idea of evolution is very old. Hunters believed that animals—and especially the ones they hunted—were, in some mysterious way, their brothers. Aristotle argued that all the forms of nature constituted a series, a chain of being, which began with the simple and became more and more complex, striving towards the perfect. In the Latin *evolution* means unfolding.

A group of handicapped patients from a local institution come into the theatre. Some have to be helped up the tiers; others manage by themselves; one or two are in wheel-chairs. They form a different kind of audience—or rather, an audience with different reactions. They are less puzzled, less astounded but more amused. Like children? Not at all. They are less puzzled, because they are more familiar with what is out of the ordinary. Or, to put it another way, their sense of the normal is far wider.

What was new and outrageous in the *Origin of the Species*, when it was first published in 1859, was Darwin's argument that all animal species had evolved from the same prototype and that this immensely slow evolution had taken place through certain accidental mutations being favoured by natural selection, which had worked according to the principle of the survival of the fittest. A series of accidents. Without design or purpose and without experience counting. (Darwin rejected Jean Baptiste Lamarck's thesis that acquired characteristics could be inherited.) The pre-condition for Darwin's theory being plausible was something even more shocking: the wastes of empty time required—about 500 million years!

Until the nineteenth century it was generally, if not universally, believed that the world was a few thousand years old—something that could be measured by the time-scale of human generations—as in the fifth chapter of Genesis. But in 1830 George Lyell published *The Principles of Geology* and proposed that the earth, with 'no vestige of a beginning—no prospect of an end' was millions, perhaps hundreds of millions of years old.

Darwin's thinking was a creative response to the terrifying immensity of what had just been revealed. And the sadness of Darwinism—for no other scientific revolution when it was made, broadcast so little hope—derived, I think, from the desolation of the distances involved. The sadness, the desolation, is there in the last sentence of *The Descent of Man*, published in 1871: 'We must, however, acknowledge, as it seems to me, that man with all his noble qualities, still bears in his bodily frame the indelible stamp of his lowly origin.' 'The indelible stamp' speaks volumes. *Indelible* in the sense that (unfortunately) it cannot be washed out. *Stamp* meaning brand, mark, stain. And in the word *lowly* during the nineteenth century, as in Britain today, there is shame.

The liberty of the newly revealed universe with its expanses of space and time brought with it a feeling of insignificance and *pudeur*, from which the best that could be redeemed was the virtue of intellectual courage, the virtue of being unflinching. And courageous the thinkers of that time were!

Whenever an actor, who is not a baby, wants to piss or shit, he or she gets up and goes to the edge of a balcony or deck and there defecates or urinates below, so as to remain clean. An habitual act which we seldom see enacted on the stage. And the effect is surprising. The public watch with a kind of pride. An altogether legitimate one.

Mostly the thinkers of the nineteenth century thought mechanically, for theirs was the century of machines. They thought in terms of chains, branches, lines, comparative anatomies, clockworks, grids. They knew about power, resistance, speed, competition. Consequently they discovered a great deal about the material world, about tools and production. What they knew less about is what we still don't know much about: the way brains work. I can't get this out of my mind: it's somewhere at the centre of the theatre we're watching.

Apes don't live entirely within the needs and impulses of their own bodies—like the cats do. (It may be different in the wild, but this is true on the stage.) They have a gratuitous curiosity. All animals play, but the others play at being themselves, whereas the apes experiment. They suffer from a surplus of curiosity. They can momentarily forget their needs and are not restricted to a single, unchanging role. A young female will pretend to be a mother cuddling a baby lent by its real mother. 'Baby-sitting' the zoologists call it.

Their surplus of curiosity, their research (every animal searches, only apes research), make them suffer in two evident ways—and probably also in others, invisibly. Their bodies, forgotten, suddenly nag, twinge and irritate. They become impatient with their own skin—like Marat suffering from eczema.

And then, too, starved of events, they suffer boredom. Baudelaire's *l'ennui*. Not at the same level of self-doubt, but nevertheless with pain, apathy. The signs of boredom may resemble those of simple drowsiness. But *l'ennui* has its unmistakable lassitude. The body, instead of relaxing, huddles; the eyes stare painfully without focus; the hands, finding nothing new to touch or do, become like gloves worn by a creature drowning.

'If it could be demonstrated,' Darwin wrote, 'that any complex organ existed which could not possibly have been formed by numerous, successive slight modifications, my theory would absolutely break down.'

If the apes are partly victims of their own bodies—the price they pay, like man, for not being confined to their immediate needs—they have found a consolation, which Europe has forgotten. My mother used to say the chimps were looking for fleas and that, when they found one, they put it between their teeth and bit it. But it goes further than Mother thought—as I guessed even then. The chimpanzees touch and caress and scratch each other for hours on end (and according to the etiquette rules of a strict group hierarchy) not only for purposes of hygiene, but to give pleasure. 'Grooming,' as it is called, is one of their principal ways of appeasing the troublesome body.

This one is scratching inside her own ear with her little finger. Now she has stopped scratching to examine minutely her small nail. Her gestures are intimately familiar and strikingly remote. (The same is true for most actions on any theatre stage.) An orang-utan is preparing a bed for herself. Suddenly she hesitates before placing her armful of straw on the floor, as if she has heard a siren. Not only are the apes' functional gestures familiar, but also their expressive ones. Gestures which denote surprise, amusement, tenderness, irritation, pleasure, indifference, desire, fear.

Their movements are different from ours. Everything which derives from the apes' skill in swinging from branches— *brachiation* as the zoologists call it—sets them apart. In evolutionary history, however, this difference is in fact a link. Monkeys walk on all fours along the tops of branches and use their tails for hanging. The common ancestors of man and apes began, instead, to use their arms—began to become *brachiators.* This gave them the advantage of being able to reach the fruit at the ends of the branches!

I must have been two years old when I had my first cuddly toy. It was a monkey. A chimpanzee, in fact. I think I called him Jackie. To be certain, I'd have to ask my mother. She would remember. But my mother is dead. There is just a chance—one in a hundred million (about the same as a chance mutation being favoured by natural selection)—that a reader may be able to tell me, for we had visitors to our home in Higham's Park, in East London, sixty years ago, and I presented my chimp to everyone

who came through the front door. I think his name was Jackie.

Slowly, the hanging position, favoured by natural selection, changed the anatomy of the *brachiators'* torsos so that finally they became half upright animals—although not yet as upright as us. It is thanks to hanging from trees that we have long collar bones which keep our arms away from our chests, wrists which allow our hands to bend backwards and sideways and shoulder sockets that let our arms rotate. It is thanks to hanging from trees that one of the actors can throw himself into the arms of a mother and now cry. Brachiation gave us breasts to beat and to be held against. No other animal can do these things.

When Darwin thought about the eyes of mammals, he admitted that he broke out in a cold sweat. The complexity of the eye was hard to explain within the logic of his theory, for it implied the co-ordination of so many evolutionary 'accidents'. If the eye is to work at all, all the elements have to be there, tear glands, eyelid, cornea, pupil, retina, millions of light-sensitive rods and cones which transmit to the brain millions of electrical impulses per second. Before they constituted an eye, these intricate parts would have been useless, so why should they have been favoured by natural selection? The existence of the eye perfidiously suggests an evolutionary aim, an intention.

Darwin finally got over the problem by going back to the existence of light-sensitive spots on one-celled organisms. These, he claimed, could have been 'the first eye' from which the evolution of our complex eyes began.

I have the impression that the oldest gorilla may be blind. Like Beckett's Pozzo. I ask his keeper, a young woman with fair hair.

Yes, she says, he's almost blind.

How old is he? I ask.

She looks at me hard. About your age, she replies, in his early sixties.

Recently, molecular biologists have shown that we share with apes ninety-nine per cent of their DNA. Only one per cent of his genetic code separates man from the chimpanzee or the gorilla. The orang-utan, which means in the language of the people of Borneo 'man of the forest,' is fractionally further removed. If we take another animal family, in order to emphasize how small the one per cent is, a dog differs from a racoon by twelve per cent. The genetic closeness between man and ape—apart from making our theatre possible—strongly suggests that their common ancestor existed, not twenty million years ago as the Neo-Darwinist palaeontologists believed, but maybe only four million years ago. This molecular evidence has been contested because there are no fossil proofs to support it. But in evolutionary theory, fossils, it seems to me, have usually been notable by their absence!

In the Anglo-Saxon world today, the Creationists, who take the Genesis story of the Creation as the literal truth, are increasingly vocal and insist that their version be taught in schools alongside the Neo-Darwinist one. The orang-utan is like he is, say the Creationists, because that's the way God made him, once and for all, five thousand years ago! He is like he is, reply the Neo-Darwinists, because he has been efficient in the ceaseless struggle for survival!

Her orang-utan eyes operate exactly like mine—each retina with its 130 million rods and cones. But her expression is the oldest I've ever seen. Approach it at your peril, for you can fall into a kind of maelstrom of ageing. The plunge is still there in Jean Mohr's photo.

Not far up the Rhine from Basel, Angelus Silesius, the seventeenth-century German Doctor of Medicine, studied in Strasbourg, and he once wrote:

Anybody who passes more than a day in eternity
is as old as God could ever be.

I look at her with her eyelids which are so pale that when she closes them they're like eye cups, and I wonder.

The conceptual framework in which the Neo-Darwinists and the Creationists debate, is of such limited imagination that the contrast with the immensity of the process whose origin they are searching, is flagrant. They are like two bands of seven-year-olds

who, having discovered a packet of love letters in an attic, try to piece together the story behind the correspondence. Both bands are ingenious and argue ferociously with one another, but the passion of the letters is beyond their competence.

Perhaps it is objectively true that only poetry can talk of birth and origin. Because true poetry invokes the whole of language (it breathes with everything it has not said), just as the origin invokes the whole of life, the whole of Being.

The mother orang-utan has come back, this time with her baby. She is sitting right up against the glass. The children in the audience have come close to watch her. Suddenly I think of a Madonna and Child by Cosimo Tura. I'm not indulging in a sentimental confusion. I haven't forgotten I'm talking about apes, any more than I've forgotten I'm watching a theatre. The more one emphasizes the millions of years, the more extraordinary the expressive gestures become. Arms, fingers, eyes, always eyes . . . A certain way of being protective, a certain gentleness—if one could feel the fingers on one's neck, one would say a certain *tenderness*—which has endured for five million years.

A species that did not protect its young would not survive comes the answer. Indisputably. But the answer does not explain the theatre.

I ask myself about the theatre—about its mystery and its essence. It's to do with time. The theatre, more tangibly than any other art, presents us with the past. Paintings may show what the past looked like, but they are like traces or foot-prints; they no longer move. With each theatre performance, what once happened is re-enacted. Each time we keep the same rendezvous: with Macbeth who can't wake up from his downfall; with Antigone who must do her duty. And each night in the theatre, Antigone, who died three millennia ago, says: 'We have only a short time to please the living, all eternity to please the dead.'

Theatre depends upon two times physically co-existing. The hour of the performance and the moment of the drama. If you read a novel, you leave the present; in the theatre you never leave the present. The past becomes the present in the only way that it is possible for this to happen. And this unique possibility is theatre.

The Creationists, like all bigots, derive their fervour from rejection—the more they can reject, the more righteous they themselves feel. The Neo-Darwinists are trapped within the machine of their theory, in which there can be no place for creation as an act of love. (Their theory was born of the nineteenth century, the most orphaned of centuries.)

The ape theatre in Basel, with its two times, suggests an alternative view. The evolutionary process unfolded, more or less as the evolutionists suppose, within time. The fabric of its duration has been stretched to breaking point by billions of years. Outside time, God is still (present tense) creating the universe.

Silesius, after he left Strasbourg, to return to Cracow, wrote: 'God is still creating the world. Does that seem strange to you? You must suppose that in him there is no before nor after, as there is here.'

How can the timeless enter the temporal? the gorilla now asks me.

Can we think of time as a field magnetized by eternity? I'm no scientist. (As I say that, I can see the real ones smiling!)

Which are they?

The ones up there on a ladder, looking for something. Now they're coming down to take a bow . . .

As I say, I'm no scientist, but I have the impression that scientists today, when dealing with phenomena, whose time or spatial scale is either immense or very small (a full set of human genes contains about six billion bases: bases being the units—the signs—of the genetic language) are on the point of breaking through space and time to discover another axis on which events may be strung, and that, in face of the hidden scales of nature, they resort increasingly to the model of a brain or mind to explain the universe.

'Can't God find what he is looking for?' To this question, Silesius replied: 'From eternity he is searching for what is lost, far from him, in time.'

The orang-utan mother presses the baby's head against her chest.

Birth begins the process of learning to be separate. The separation is hard to believe or accept. Yet, as we accept it, our imagination grows—imagination which is the capacity to re-connect, to bring together, that which is separate. Metaphor finds the traces which indicate that all is one. Acts of solidarity, compassion, self-sacrifice, generosity are attempts to re-establish— or at least a refusal to forget—a once-known unity. Death is the hardest test of accepting the separation which life has incurred.

You're playing with words!

Who said that?

Jackie!

The act of creation implies a separation. Something that remains attached to the creator is only half created. To create is to let take over something which did not exist before and is therefore new. And the new is inseparable from pain, for it is alone.

One of the male chimps is suddenly angry. Histrionically. Everything he can pick up, he throws. He tries to pull down the stage trees. He is like Samson at the temple. But unlike Samson, he is not high up in the group hierarchy of the cage. The other actors are none the less impressed by his fury.

Alone, we are forced to recognize that we have been created, like everything else. Only our souls, when encouraged, remember the origin, wordlessly.

Silesius's master was Johannes Eckhardt, who, further down the Rhine beyond Strasbourg, in Cologne, wrote during the thirteenth century: 'God becomes God when the animals say: God.'

Are these the words which the play, behind the sound-proof plate glass, is about?

In any case, I can't find better.

JAYNE ANNE PHILLIPS
IN SUMMER CAMPS

Concede the heat of noon in summer camps. The quarters wavering in bottled heat, cots lined up in the big dark rooms that are pitch black if you walk in out of the sun. Black, quiet, empty, and the screen door banging shut three times behind you. Allowed in alone only if you are faint. Perhaps the heat has come over you, settled in from above and sucked your insides until you must lie down to sleep in the empty cabin while the rest are at hiking or canoes or archery. Now you lie there sleeping and the room is heavy and warm, but cooler than noon, the rough wooden walls exuding shade. The cots are precisely mute. Identical and different in olive green blankets, each pulled tight and tucked. In your mind, you see the bodies lying there, each in its own future. You are frightened because it is you here with the future. And they are scattered along Mud River walk, obscured by dense leaves, their occasional cries no louder than the sounds of the invisible birds. Or they are standing in line before bright targets stretched across baled hay. They are holding taut bows straight out, pulling back on the strings with all their strength.

Lenny

The sky burned white to blond to powder to an almighty blue; the sun fell unobstructed. The girls wore heavy green shorts that were too long and short-sleeved white blouses embroidered in a clover silhouette above the right breast. The blouses were all too big; only the older girls with larger breasts looked strangely seductive in them. The shorts were dark, forest green gabardine, fluted with fine yellow braid on two deep pockets. In Charleston, the state headquarters of Girl Guides did not concede the heat of the Appalachian summer; they recommended knee socks with garters, neck ties with gold pins at the throats, wool berets. But Greenbriar Camp was newly re-opened, the cabins were in shored-up disrepair, the cots themselves cast-offs from a Boy Scout camp in the Panhandle. The county was low-income, the mines, state-wide, laid off. Only the shorts and blouses were regulation; girls on Supplement or Full Supplement wore second-

Photo: Ralph Eugene Meatyard

167

hand uniforms and got away with rolling up their sleeves.

The upper sites had no cabins at all, just tents donated by the Veterans of Foreign Wars. The tents were war surplus, Army olive, weathered, alight on squat frames that were new and rough. Each frame seemed the unfinished skeleton of some more ambitious structure. Pale two-by-fours angled out from the canvas tent sides like rows of awkward elbows; each held a lashed knot tight and the square form of the tent remained uncomfortably aloft. The raised front flaps were tied back, revealing olive interiors so completely plain that the metal cots with their blue-striped mattresses looked direly ornamental. The plank floors tilted and some were supported by posts in front or behind. Lenny and Cap were in the last row of Highest; beyond the rear wall of their tent, the world dropped off. Tattered in the descending bank, brush and flowers grew waist-high. Lenny had stood there, looking up. From behind, the tents looked temporary and strange. Like the odd dwellings of nomads in flight from floods, they perched on the hillsides in ever ascending order. Enclaves meant to be A, B and C camps were soon dubbed High, Higher and Highest: Girl Guides were rotated ever higher, the better to experience lashing in the wild, and long hikes to flag-raising. Seniors at Highest camp walked provisions up every morning after early swim in Mud River, and were never seen except at breakfast and at seven a.m. formation. Lenny and Cap stood then in a single line with the rest, just round the flag, looking hard and scratched in their dark, wrinkled bermudas as the Juniors struggled out of the woods. The Seniors wore slouchy beige or white hats and terry cloth wrist bands: marks of combat with the insects and the heat, and the mist they were already walking through when reveille sounded far below at the quad. The dew-slick windings that were the trails from Highest were a jungle unto themselves and smelled of melons and snakes. All day, Lenny was a Senior with the Seniors. What did they do up there? *A million things*, Lenny had lied to her sister, Alma, who was only a Junior and slept in a civilized cabin off the quad. At night the Seniors sang. They were made to sing. From below, their fires would appear as haphazard orange winks in the dark, and Lenny knew their voices carried as vague chants that lifted and dropped: Come by here, my Lord. Maybe they were praying.

After cooking and mess duty and campfire close, they finally went to their tents, each one a canvas bunker whose sides and drooping roof held the heat of the day. Lenny and Cap were on the side of the mountain; if they tied up the front and rear flaps, air moved through the tent like a blessing. At ten and eleven they were still awake, indolent, murmuring, lying on narrow cots with the sheets still tucked. Cap wore her underwear but Lenny took off everything, relieved to be rid at last of the blouse that buttoned to the neck, the heavy shorts that covered her to her knees. She lay on her bed, legs spread, arms out, her blond hair flung over her face. Her hair, weighty, dense, released from its binding elastic, smelled of woodsmoke but felt cool; she imagined its light colour made it cool in the dark of night on Highest. Even the lanterns were out. The counsellors were sleeping, having made up chore lists for tomorrow; in these hours, Lenny was free. She felt her body borne up and slowly spinning, spun free by the cooling air, the blackness, the night sounds that grew louder and louder as she concentrated on each one: crickets emitting their pierced warbles, the woods owls hooting like they were trying to get breath, the grasses moving ever so slightly, crack of a twig. Though she complained, Lenny liked camp; she liked being dirty, dousing a change of uniform in the stream, throwing it over a rope line to dry and putting it on still damp. She liked the fact that there were no boys, just Buddy, the cook's little kid, who followed her everywhere she went, and Frank, the good-looking bugler, perhaps a year older than they, safely observed from a distance. There were four or five workmen, faceless in khaki clothes, their river enclave of ditches and pipes unreal as home. Camp was a simple map. Lenny liked the endless walking that was by now automatic, the meaningless, inarguable up and down of the mountain. The routine, the common movements of the group, were oddly pleasant: nothing to be thought of, nothing to be decided, only this chore or that chore, all of them alike, really, the cleaning of objects, the storage of objects, the carrying up and down the mountain of objects. Even food seemed a series of objects, peeled and cut and cooked into mash, even the water to cook it hauled from somewhere. All day Lenny carried this or that—apples, potatoes, buckets, wood—through wavery heat, conscious sometimes of the heat as a nearly liquid element, as though they were all kept upright, forced to move by what oppressed them. They struggled against it as swimmers struggle, cutting through, buoyed up. The days were long. When dark descended, Lenny felt cooled and numb. She thought of the glass of beer in her father's hand: she felt as transparent and dense. He would be drinking beer now, on the dark porch at home, in the absolute quiet of Alma's and Lenny's absence, Audrey a cancelled zero somewhere in the workings of the house. Lenny couldn't imagine her mother except in the context of Alma and herself; her father she saw clearly. Wes existed apart from them, always, that was Audrey's constant reproach. Home nights, Lenny often walked outside with a paper cup and Wes would pour her part of his beer; she drank it down in slow swallows and it spread through her. At night in Greenbriar Camp, protected by Cap and dozens of sleeping strangers, she imagined the beer pouring into her and over her, thick and golden like cold, syrupy lava, poured from her father's glass in a technicolor dream. She wasn't here with Cap, she wasn't anywhere. In the emptiness, full, she nearly slept but didn't sleep, and floated.

'Lenny, you can hear them.' Cap moved on her bed. 'They're flying.'

'What, the owls?'

'No, listen—like whistling rattles, but they zoom close and go away. Bats. They must live down near the river, but how could they?'

'There aren't bats. If there was even a chance, the counsellors would be wearing protective clothing after dark. Suits of armour.'

Cap laughed her gravelly, private laugh. 'Lenore, aren't you scared, lying naked like that? What if the bats swarm in and cover you with their rat bodies and their little claws and their crackly wings?' She crawled silently from her bed and lay full length on the wood plank floor, her face at the edge, peering out into darkness. 'Last night I thought I saw them, but there was no moon and they vanished too fast. Tonight we'll see them, at the tops of the trees, where the light is strongest.'

'What light? All I see is the light of those white underpants of yours.'

Lenny thought of crawling quietly on to Cap's back and sleeping on top of her, letting her weight settle in. She didn't know why she had such thoughts; somehow, at camp, Cap had become as familiar, ever-present, owned, as Alma at home. There to be touched and shoved and moved and irritated, except it was Cap, not Alma, Cap, who was stronger and a little shorter than Lenny, whose freckled skin smelled of some velvet woods creature, whose breath smelled enticingly of tobacco, who stole cigarettes from purses. They were both fourteen but Cap was older by several months; her face was browned from the sun and her eyes looked lighter now, gray as slate and hard. Cap, whose father was Mr Briarley of Consol Coal, lived in Gaither in a big house with a maid. She slept in a canopy bed. Lenore had slept there with her, under a kind of ruffled ceiling. Here in the night green drab of the tent, in the woods, along the trails, in the institution of the routine, they were a team, cut loose from the safe things that separated them. Lenore teased and held back but Cap smiled, breathing *at your service* or *Queen Lenore the Unconscious*; she shoved back and made all the games more fun. She liked baiting Lenny, she dared her to wrestle, she laughed and plotted pranks that were never carried out, just talked about in the dark in wild, interesting words, curses Cap said her father yelled at her mother. In the dark, she whispered in sibilant tones that sounded like another language, very fast and harsh. She affected a Natasha accent from the Bullwinkle cartoons but made it delicious and threatening, squinting her eyes, moving her hands as though to ward off cobwebs. She was powerful, off on her own in a society she could circumvent, but her power supported Lenore—Lenore could daydream or forget, shirk some duty, and Cap would take up the slack, finish for her, do it for her. She was 'of service' but she wanted something back. Lenore was only waiting to find out what it was.

'Lenny, I see them. They're eating the clouds of gnats that come out of the weeds at night. Quick, you can see them.' Cap felt for Lenny's arm and pulled.

'All right.' Lenore hated to get up when she was floating, but she stood upright and the feeling stayed with her. She got to her knees, then lay down with her chin at the edge of the flooring. Cap touched Lenny's face, turning her head and pointing down at the crown of the trees below them. Just on the surface of the foliage, shadows fluttered. The shadows rose higher and took form, scraps of black paper, shaken angrily, gaining the air in spasms.

'*Look* at them,' Cap whispered.

For an instant, naked, Lenny was paralyzed with surprise. Her skin tingled as though a veil had been pulled across her flesh. The bats moved, their flight inherently terrifying in its speed, its inhuman tremor. The night looked navy blue, round as a deep plate. The bats were soot and remnants, emitting the shrill, silent screams of their community. Then pieces of the mosaic dropped suddenly and swooped, lifted and were gone, flown back over Highest to the north.

Dimly, Lenny heard Cap murmuring and felt her wrist wetted and warmed. Cap held it in her mouth as a dog holds damaged prey, teeth resting on the flesh just hard enough to make an impression. Instinctively, Lenny kicked and swung, felt herself released, Cap's misplaced slap at her face landing in her neck. Cap left her hand there and grasped Lenny's hair. 'Take it easy, Lenore, I was joking. They're just bats.'

'Well, I never saw them before,' Lenny spat back. 'I've never seen them, they're not like birds at all, they're horrible.'

'OK, OK, forget you saw them. Who said they were like birds? They're vermin.'

'Oh, be quiet. Can't you stop showing me things? Leave me alone.'

'Sure thing.' Cap hissed the words and rose from the floor in one movement. Her bed creaked when she sat, then she sighed, betraying herself.

Listening, Lenore was frightened again. 'Let's go, let's go down the mountain. I can't sleep now, because of you. You have to come too.'

'What?'

'No one will even know we left. We can go down here, right off the edge of the tent, circle around to the woods trail and go down to Turtle Hole. We can swim and be back in an hour.'

'Lenore, I don't want to put my clothes back on and walk all the way down there.'

'Yes, you do. I can tell you do.'

'I'll only do it,' she laughed, 'if you'll go just as you are now.'

'Don't be dumb. The brush off this way is full of briars.'

'All right. But once we get on the trail, you have to take off everything but your shoes.' Already, she was putting on her clothes, fighting her way into a T-shirt.

Lenore tossed her head defiantly, like at home, even though no one was watching. 'Fine. I don't care. There's no one on the trail. But when we get to the water, you have to go in too. Both of us.'

'Oh, in that mud bottom, when you can even touch the bottom! You sink to your ankles . . . I'll have to tread water, I can't bear it!' She stage-whispered, her Natasha accent drunkenly precise.

Zippers, tying of laces, double-knots at the ends, no slipping in the dark dark dark of Highest trail. Cap opened the footlocker to find the flashlight but Lenny shushed her and closed the heavy lid—no light, she signalled, cat's eyes, night vision, see in the tunnel, radar, laser light—anyway, someone would see a flashlight beam, suddenly cutting across the trail.

'You first.' Cap motioned towards the edge.

They squatted and Lenny was over first. The slender pole, central support propping the tent floor, smelled of dirt. The rubber soles of Lenny's sneakers slowed her short descent and when she was down, she looked up. Peculiar feeling, like spying under someone's secret room; the board floor with its wide slats showed space between the lengths, as though the ground illuminated upward.

Exhilarated, Lenny turned and ran, lifting her knees high to skirt the briars, plundering the smell and the wetness. Grasses ripped as she moved. Little by little, she could see. She touched with her fingertips the wet umbrellaed tops of Queen Anne's lace, heard the briars catch at her, didn't feel them. Ahead the furzy towering shapes of the trees sheltered Highest trail, a few hundred feet down from the tents. All the rest were sleeping! And this was better than a dream. Lenny gained the trail and stopped. The dirt felt softer, more velvet, dew had wet it. The world looked softened, night-furred; the depths of the woods were an odd black shot with deep green. Still, she could discern every shape. Silently, the branches of trees moved as they never moved in daylight, weighted with heat. There was a wind rippling them, a wind like a breath blown through the woods from start to finish. She pulled off her shirt and shorts and threw them down. There, the air was on her. She stood at attention, listening with her skin. Years ago, they'd let her go shirtless in the summer, like a boy. It had felt like this, catching the blinkering fireflies in bottles, but not so good. Cap was beside her, breathing as though she'd jumped on to the trail from a high place, dropped down from the limbs of the trees. She picked up Lenny's clothes and threw them to the side of the trail, then shoved. They were running, skip, stub, touch the rock sides of the slanted earth, touching with their shoes each big stone they skirted in daylight. Going down in darkness was fast, unbelievably fast, no sound but their breath, hut hut hut as though someone softly punched them as they dropped.

They heard the stream before they saw it; here was where they washed dishes and pots, dunked their sweaty clothes, gulped handfuls of water so cold it stung. The stream tumbled down the mountain to join Mud River, widened, widened, flattened finally at the bottom of the hill and grew slow. Just before it joined the river it flowed over its former banks, dammed by a deserted beaver dam and fallen trees. The beaver dam still stood, a dike of branches and crumbling mud. Whatever washed down through the stream came to rest against it; no one walked or swam too close. There were a few bottles or cans, some of them broken, and the occasional odd, desolate bit of clothing: an old boot, a lady's glove. Then there was the river, wide as a three-lane road, and the trail alongside like an afterthought. Ahead Lenny could make out the swinging bridge, still and elemental in the dark. Moonlight caught one edge and glistened the shape; it hung there like a woman's necklace. Lenny wanted to start across but Cap took her arm and urged her further up along the boundary of the woods—the opposite bank had been torn up by the workmen laying pipe. At night the scarred ground and dirt piles, the tubular mounds of iron, seemed an abandoned desecration. On this side, further along the river, the trail split off through the woods to Turtle Hole. Here, at the edge of camp property, the country people swam when camp was not in session, diving from a flat boulder that overhung the water. Girl Guides didn't swim there, which was odd, as the water was a perfect silver oval, deep in the centre. Maybe there were snapping turtles, or ghosts. How would it look at night? Lenny wanted to see. The bridge moved as though trod upon, and shimmered as they left it behind.

Threading their way along the narrow river bank, they were Indian scouts, moving as though pursued, scrambling precisely. Cap was first, a certain shield. Lenore consciously echoed her movements, crouching, swooping, standing taller and striding; naked, she felt like a clean white cloth, a rippling slipstream. She saw her own glowing legs move reliably over the dark ground and stayed in tandem, Cap's shadow, secret, invisible even to her, unknown. Cap would move fast and go far—Lenny imagined following, unseen, to distant times and places, places most people from Gaither would never go. An understanding struck Lenore wordlessly; Cap had arrived in Gaither only to find Lenore. That's why she was here where she didn't belong. Even now, Lenny felt crowds watching them, rows of silent presence, and she turned her head to see the glower of the trees, row upon row of staggered slender shapes. Second-growth maples, oaks, ash, the trees held upright their densely leaved bouquets. Only the knobby beginnings of branches were visible under the foliage, as though a few thin arms supported these masses of minutely stirred leaves. Lenny moved quickly and her rapidly changing perspective lent the trees a semblance of movement as subtle as the shifting of an eye. The forest was not like rocks or sticks, it was *alive*. She had never really known before.

They had left the river behind and were moving through the woods, almost to Turtle Hole. Cap slowed and crouched down. Lenny was impatient. Now she could see the water, perfect, silver and contained.

'Be quiet,' Cap whispered. 'There's someone here, up high, on the rock.' She lowered herself into the tall reeds along the border of the woods and they both sat, peering through stalks.

'Is it Buddy, wandering around at night?' Lenore saw no one.

'No, he wouldn't be out this late. No, it's a man.' She sighed intently.

They both moved forward carefully, nearly to the edge of the water. Lenore listened. She heard movement, the quiet clank of something metal. A hunched form sat on the flat slab of boulder that overhung the water. Then the form straightened and pointed an immensely long, thin finger into the night sky. The finger cracked and whistled, flinging an invisible line far out.

'He's fishing,' Cap said.

The line had landed and sunk its weighted hook. Soundless, concentric echoes widened across the breadth of the water. The surface looked placid and heavy, glistened with dull particles of light. By day Turtle Hole was just the dull green of a turtle's horny flesh; now it was different, and the mute border of the trees was black. The form sat quietly, holding the long pole. He was dressed in dark pants—he wore no shirt but Lenny saw the glint of a belt buckle. He turned and settled, leaning against a large stone. They could make out his staring face, his eyes fixed on the water.

'Frank,' Lenny breathed. Here was where he came at night, probably every night. She knew of him suddenly, days at his camp site, sleeping miserably in the drowsy heat, appearing to play reveille and taps, to mow the grassy quad with the old push mower. His wrinkled clothes. Sometimes he wore a billed hat. He noticed none of them. They were beneath his notice because this is where he lived while the rest of them were dead in their swoony sleep. No one told him what to do. He was alone.

Cap touched Lenore, and pointed. Not speaking, they inched closer, careful to stay concealed. The grasses smelled pungent and were sharp; Lenny felt them trailing over her skin and knew they tasted sour. Through the reeds, she could see him. He moved his head, not hearing them but sensing an approach. They stopped, perhaps thirty feet to his right.

Lenny knew she would stand and make him see her. She felt dulled, heavy with urgency, like an insect pinned to paper, trying to beat its wings. She heard the low yearning bleats of crickets and wanted to walk straight towards him. She must have begun to stand.

Cap stopped her with a whisper. 'No, let him see me first.' She stood soundlessly, waiting for him to find her. Lenore crouched, her head level with Cap's knees. She gazed up the length of Cap's long body and remembered her mother's bare arms in summer, how large Audrey had seemed, a giant at the screen door of the kitchen, how the door whammed shut with a slash, cutting the air like a weapon. The concrete stoop beyond was lit up by the angle of the sun, its nubby surface embedded with shards of glitter. Lenny felt herself momentarily blinded by those dazzling mornings, as though a light were switched on in the dark, but it was night now, and in fact the night sky was pricked with stars far above Cap's shoulders. The stars were endless, faceted and glowing. Like fireworks, they had exploded into the sky and were still receding, falling and burning.

'He saw me,' someone said, and Cap had knelt back into the grass. She was untying Lenny's sneakers. Lenore shifted her weight and the shoes were gently pulled away. The water was close and the ground was damp.

Hidden, Lenny felt powerful and safe. But he had seen them; he had put down the pole and was looking into the dark, empty air above the grasses. No motion, no sound. The feeling would crumble and burn up, like the stars, unless she moved. Whoever, whatever he was, she felt herself hurtling towards him. She held him in her gaze and stood. The air was vast as outer space, and warm. She couldn't read his eyes, his expression, he was only a form, standing, beginning to move. The water was an oblong egg holding more light than the night could hold, and she moved towards it. She couldn't feel the ground. Her feet, her legs, were pleasantly numb, tingling, but her hands stung with heat and she opened them. She waded into the water to be held up, but the water, to her waist, to her breasts, was not heavy enough to help. She saw him slip into the pond in his baggy pants, moving towards her, and she only wanted him to hurry. The water broke around him and the sound of its crack and gentle roll seemed delayed, like thunder after mile-high lightning. She had to open her mouth to breathe.

Suddenly he was close, his face, his eyes. He didn't recognize her, he had never seen her before and perhaps didn't see her now; she was safe and she opened her arms to him. He didn't seem like Frank, the boy they'd watched. So near, he was almost a man; his hands were broad and flat, his shoulders squared at her forehead. She stroked him and felt his muscles tense as though her touch were electric. He was ready and he was afraid. His open palms on her nipples were a soft pressure meant to confirm her nakedness but she moved forward and up and made him support her weight. She couldn't stand; she wanted to close her eyes and hold on. Her head was above his now, her face in his hair. He was unbearably fragrant, like flowers and dust, and his thick dry hair was warm. He nuzzled inside, between her breasts, like a vicious baby, pushing, using his mouth. He moved his hands, lifting her against him, sucked at her skin, her throat, tasting until he found her lips. She had never really kissed anyone but her parents and girlfriends; it wasn't what she had thought. It was more like eating, eating something swollen and sweet that you could taste but never swallow, never have. She was feeding him, filling him up, but he couldn't pull her close enough. He pushed deeper with his tongue, slower, pulling her tighter the length of their bodies. His hands grew frantic, moving haphazardly over her; their panic began to pull everything into focus. Lenore felt a core of blurry fear almost coalesce but then Cap was in the water near them, touching them both, circling round them, her mouth on his neck, his ears, as though she were whispering. He was breathing quickly, trying to move them toward the bank, but Cap held Lenore against him, touching the backs of Lenny's thighs, urging her closer so that Lenny opened her legs and clasped his waist. His hands found her hips and she touched the hard buckle of his belt, pressed her hand close under it, inside. When she touched him he froze and made a sound that started a throbbing pain in her. She nearly moved to touch herself but felt a hand hard against her. She felt it probe inside and let her weight rest there, then she clasped him tighter and stopped thinking. His mouth was on hers but she pulled away, gasping; she had to cry out, then she couldn't stop her voice. Shattering, she heard a coarse, continuous moaning as she turned, over and over, tumbling through some pierced and narrow space. She felt a hot rush and knew she was urinating, emptying into the hand that held her. She let that warmth happen and the turning eased. Tears filled her eyes as he stiffened against her. She wanted to hold him but Cap was between them, urging her back. Lenny remembered the water again as an element separate from herself; she could taste it, smell it. She wanted to sleep in it, let herself sink. Her feet touched the mud bottom and Cap was pulling her away. They moved together, escaping before anything was said, before he heard their voices or truly saw them. They were at the water's edge before they heard him call to them. They ran, throwing water off their long bodies, forgetting Lenny's shoes in the tall reeds, stumbling until they gained the path. The woods stretched before them, dense, connected shapes surprisingly the same, but the colour of the night had altered.

In the Shack at Night: Parson

At night the shack was darker even than the night beyond it, and when he first lay down on his pallet he felt himself cosseted within some creature whose existence he had always suspected. He seemed to be in utter darkness, the dark that is in the inner guts of living things, and he listened for a heartbeat and heard it, a pounding on a wall, a wrenching pump pump pump that was wet and sick, and gradually the close, furry dark took on a bit of the light of the open night, the night in the forest. Out there the sky looked paler than the trees, which were so black they had no depth, and palest of all was the glassy surface of Turtle Hole, which he could see through the two windows of the front wall of the shack. A week ago he'd torn down the tar-paper covering the cracked glass: Turtle Hole lay forward and to the right. From deep in the overhanging trees he glimpsed its opaque light. The water was roundly lop-sided like a bowl squashed flat, the water was motionless like night ice that still might tremble if some creature swam beneath the perfect surface, the water scared him mightily and so he lay very still, he lay there and the space of the shack enlarged. Floater, underling, he clung to an udder of charcoal dark and saw the steep pitch of the shack roof above him, weathered grey of the boards pale against tar-paper. Someone else had stayed here, stuffed paper between the boards, nailed up a few wood scraps in the corner where the slant was worst. Must have been a chicken coop, with a roosting shelf some tramp had long ago made into a bed. Now the partition boards were gone and the shelf built up with straw, straw he smelt chickens in, an old dust of powder and feathers, he'd sooner bed with rats than chickens, he'd killed rats many a time, shot them with a revolver when he was Preacher's boy. But chickens made him scared, the way they bobbed and pecked, jerking here and there on devilish horned feet, blinking their raw, pink eyes that were stupid and soulless as the eyes of fish. The noise they made, the *bwak, bwak* cut and cluck, the *ck ck ck* that stammered and froze his blood, how he used to have to chop their heads off at Pruntytown, stand there and hold the bloody hatchet while their headless bodies flopped and staggered like runt machines. They were evil, the way they couldn't die, they might have made him evil too, kitchen matron quarrelling at him, go on out there and pick up them birds, big boy like you scared of chickens, you gonna eat it you better be ready to kill it, but he didn't eat it, never did, he didn't want that flesh inside him even when his guts rolled with hunger. Oh it was dark inside him, he knew he was born dark and he liked to be in the daytime, in the dark he had to lie still and watch. He told himself everything evil was long gone from here, summers and winters the shack had been empty, falling down for years, who knew how many, maybe as far back as when he was with Preacher, sermonizing, fourteen years old, cow-lick and a swarth of beard, in need of a haircut and clothes, in need of a home, Preacher would say from the pulpit. And Preacher's foster son would preach on Fridays, sweating, Bible in his hand, and while he was shouting there were snakes moulting here in this abandoned slant of boards, he'd found skins, some of them so old they fell to dust when he lifted them out of leaves and dirt. Whatever he found that was good he put beneath his pallet, the dry leaves, an empty honeycomb, the clean bones of small animals rotted and returned to powders, and the snakeskins. There were rags of blankets left by vagrants, men who must have slept here in winter when the camp was closed. And since he'd gotten work on the pipe crew, the directoress, a fat red-headed woman white as pink-tinged chalk, had sent him twice to the dump with a truckload of junk. Now he had a metal kitchen chair with a ripped plastic seat, and a cot mattress discoloured and torn, softer under him than any bed he remembered. He had magazines. He had a dish with a blue flower on it, and a bucket with no handle he filled at Turtle Hole near dusk. Kneeling to fill it he saw his own face wavering and broken on the cool surface, sometimes he splattered the image with his hand, with his face, biting water that tasted clean and cut like glass, cold and brilliant, and when he came up sputtering he heard the girls singing in their camps, the sounds vague and high, mesmerizing, every night they sang and he could never hear the words, there were different words from different directions and their nonsensical rise and fall seemed to call and answer, calling him, answering, and he knew he'd come to the right place, he'd followed Carmody and come to a place he was meant to find. It almost didn't matter who he followed, any of them, fallen, vicious in their minds, could lead him to Grace.

But he'd watched Carmody carefully. Carmody, long and lank, his faded, wheat-coloured hair and squinty eyes, his face that was not young with its callow, unfinished look, showing always an edge of the rabbity, scared anger that caused him to hang back, scheming while his cohorts strutted and preened. He moved, not seeming to move, planned while he appeared to sleep: Parson dreamed he was water, an elongated, flattened sheen not unlike Turtle Hole in colour and brilliance, an oval water that moved along the edges of things like a shade or a ghost, a water that moved up walls, through bars, edged past the warrens of cells along the main corridor of the prison, water that was glistened and flat, featureless, probing, searching to take on any shape, any colour, anything to get out. For some of them, prison was no worse than what they'd lived through. But prison broke Carmody up, he was wild to finish his time, afraid of the wardens, afraid of the other men. He even seemed afraid of his wife and kid, or afraid to see them, the wife a big woman gone to fat and the kid a pale tow-head, quick and thin, darting beside her like a shadow tethered to a string. Before their rare visits Carmody was jumpy, he said his old lady was a nut for God, she and Parson would get on, but Parson wasn't much for women, was he, and Carmody laughed. Parson could smell the fear on him, a bitter vegetable smell like rotted seeds and pulp. For a while they'd shared a cell in B block: Carmody flowed from one side to the other, pacing in the dark, ranting about the block bosses and their gofers until he knelt in the corner and beat at the wall with his fist, a rhythmic pounding punctuated by frantic whispers, I gotta be a good boy, good boy, gotta be a good boy, *kill* them, *fuck* them, until Parson dragged him by the back of his shirt over to the bunks and prayed over him. Oh Christ, Carmody would mutter, struggle like a cat in a sack, shut up you crazy loon, they all know you're crazy, why the hell do you think they leave you alone? But the praying always worked and Parson was strong enough to hold him still until he calmed, hold him in the healing grip of the heavenly Father and press hard against the evil, press hard and shake the Devil loose.

In the shack at night, Parson could hear the Devil walk, stalking spirits in the vaporous air. The Devil made a scrunching sound in the grasses and leaves and loose dirt, a sound like a creature with tiny feet, and there was the airy, slick *whish* of the Devil's probing tongue, tasting and wanting, just on the other side of the thin board wall. The mist of Turtle Hole was like wet smoke in the hours before dawn. In those hours Parson had to stay awake to pray, his was a consecrated soul, no matter that the Devil slithered and wandered, sniffing at the corners of the boards, picking away with his bony, glowing fingers at the rotting wood. Parson prayed the old prayers, ones he'd learned when Preacher called him parson boy and made him kneel to speak.

Those prayers were words and more than words, flailing chants that set the air to humming, made it thick, kept the Devil pressed back beyond the boundaries of the Kingdom, back where the Devil moaned and cried, outcast, betrayed, and Preacher rattled on like a man wielding chains and whips. Back then Parson lay in his bed in the wooden house by the river in Calvary, not thirty miles from Pruntytown and the Industrial School for Boys where he'd spent the last four years. He lay in bed in his closet room behind the small kitchen and listened to Preacher pray alone in the parlour furnished with folding chairs, chairs filled three meetings a week with Christ's pilgrims. Phrases cut and slashed across Parson's vision like colours and worked their way into his sleep, *Hear ye Jerusalem! cast out your sinners and entreat your guests, fatted in the blood of the lamb and the gristled sheep, slick with the liquid gold of the Devil's songs, O hear ye fatted calves whose hooves are the Devil's cloven shoes, Unmask yourselves, fall down* . . . Parson mouthed the cadences of the lines and forgot what his name had been before, at the orphanage in Huntington, the city and the dingy park, at the foster homes where he'd always just arrived or was preparing to leave until the last, the one where he'd set the house on fire to get away and old Mr Harkness had died, stone drunk on the bathroom floor, where he'd staggered from Parson's bed. Harkness was one of the Devil's weaker servants, but foster homes for older kids were hard to come by in the coal towns, and the social workers sometimes placed boys with a widower on a farm. The case worker called Harkness, rheumy-eyed and sober, *the picture of sincerity*; Parson had been there four months, along with another boy of six or seven who never talked, just ate his rice and beans and grits and boiled chicken at Harkness's scarred table without looking up. There was the familiar mud of the country winter and the hogs and the three goats to milk, and that was all right, the goats were warm and quick. Their strange vertical pupils scared the little kid, who tailed along after Parson regardless, eager to be outside because Harkness was in the kitchen, drinking. After dark he took his transfusions out of the tin cup that hung by the door on a hook; even then he didn't hit them, he staggered, cooking suppers, and reeled around in the rooms after they'd gone upstairs. Later he came up, crying a little or whimpering, and lay down fully clothed on their beds. The little boy slept under his bed on the floor but Parson lay wrapped in his blankets, motionless under Harkness's tentative, cautious touch until the old man fell asleep or stumbled away, afraid. Now in the shack at night Parson watched the shapely dark congeal into faces, all their powerful faces, his succession of keepers and parents. Harkness wasn't the worst of them but he was helpless, sober all morning at his half-time job as a postal worker, offering his apologetic grin, seeing their clothes were clean and making a show of buying new school books instead of used ones. The night of the fire was cold and Harkness's cold face felt dead, used and stretched like putty; his mouth and the smell of the whiskey were on Parson's ears and neck. Harkness begged to get into the blankets and did, then walked to the bathroom, fell down. Parson got up then and went downstairs. There were still hot coals in the fireplace and he pulled the iron grate across the bricks to the rug, and the rug caught and began to blaze. It was warm quickly and there was a lot of light, and Parson went back up and pulled the kid from under the bed and they went out the bathroom window, walking over Harkness, and as they slid down the roof they could feel it was already hot, and smoke came off the shingles. The kid said they'd better get the goats out, since the barn was attached to the house. They did and the goats went off, clattering their hooves over dry leaves in the dark. The boys watched the fire from the edge of the woods. They weren't even cold, the old place made such flames, and later at the police station there was a Christmas tree on the desk. Parson told them he made the fire but no one believed him, and the kid said nothing. Parson said other things, how the Devil had licked his ears and breathed on him with his sick breath and begged to get warm. Then he was sent to Pruntytown and the psychologist found out he couldn't read. He'd learned, decoding old texts no longer used by the county schools, a few words to a page with pictures of the blond children and the spotted dog. Run, Spot, run! Betty throws the ball! Beyond the brick façade of the school the winter sky was low-slung and yellow. Scrub pine edged the hills, gnarled and overgrown, crushed by the weight of the cold, the damp that smelled of decaying straw. Parson read Bible stories from a children's book and went to the prayer meetings run by Preacher Summers, the volunteer revivalist from Calvary. Everyone called him Preacher. In chapel he turned the lights up bright, then prayed in the dark; once in a downpour he opened the windows wide to hear the sound. *There is the cleansing thunder of the Lord! Among you are souls bound for God, chosen to recognize the enemies of the Lord and cast them out—The wind may tear the clothes from your backs, the multitude may call you infidel, but the Lord's child never wavers.*

Here at the camp Parson wore khaki work clothes distributed to the pipe crew by the foreman. He was in disguise, just as at prison. In the shack at night Parson saw the dead, shades of the vapour world, and shades of the living who were marked for death. Carmody leered his snide joke of a grin, lounging along the low wall in prison blues. Where you from? You from up in my country? What you in for? He laughed, and his laughter was too long and slow. You not saying, or don't know, maybe. They say you ought to be over at Longwood, locked up with the loons. Carmody's mocking words were drawn out like the sounds on Preacher's old Victrola when Preacher lay his finger on a record to slow the sound of the hymn, distort it to a garbled rumble. *The Devil speaks in many guises, but this is the sound of his dark, sick soul. Never pity those who are sick with evil.* The darkness in the shack swelled a little around Preacher's words, rippled, shivered like the skin of a horse. Carmody rippled too. Along the angled ceiling Harkness floated in his ill-kempt dark blue uniform, whimpered like a dog half-froze, kicked with his feet as though he were trying to swim. But the river was a ways through the trees and Turtle Hole was too perfect to admit such desolation. Harkness began a low buzzing like a fly trapped in a screen, and Parson slept.

He awoke in witch's light, the light of the Devil's love, night light made luminous by moonglow and mist rising off the water. Now the night was coolest and Turtle Hole, warmed by the sun, drifted a moist, low-lying cloud. Moonsmoke, Preacher had said, smelling the air in Calvary, where a stream behind the rickety wooden porch of the house charged the air with a similar languid wet on summer nights. Where was Preacher now? Dead and rotted, and Parson woke at this hour, always, near midnight, rolling up towards consciousness the way words rolled up on the bottom of a plastic 8 ball Preacher had kept at his house. It's how prayer moves, he'd say, cloudy and clear, come and go; waking those years, Parson often heard him reading aloud, conversing with a heavenly ghost. Later in prison Parson woke to nothing, dead air, the men rocked shut like rocks. Here the air was so alive it tingled, alive with all of them, all the children breathing their milky sleep, pearling the night with their breath. It was a kind of heaven he'd found and the evil that could hurt them was great, it would be an evil unafraid of innocence, an evil thriving as shadow of every gesture and desire, every future. Time moved that way, and disease, and fire ate that way, catching the edge and burning towards the centre. Burning to follow Carmody, find him, Parson had waited a week after Carmody's parole, then walked off a work detail, easily, carefully, overlooked after eight years as a slow and powerful child, content, dementedly religious, afraid of the outside. He'd walked off with just the clothes he wore, his Bible strapped to his stomach under his shirt, walked the first few miles, his prison blues not so different from any labourer's clothes. A trucker at a gas station gave him a ride straight out of Carolina, gave him a map. Parson found a half-familiar cluster of names and marked those names as he was marked, with the cross of the Lord. Winfield, Bellington, Gaither, were there, town names printed smaller and smaller, and the camp, Greenbriar, set off as a small pastel square, a forest preserve, yes, preserved, in the northern part of the state. Carmody had said he lived at Greenbriar, hell no, wasn't no town, just a dirt road and a few hicks, each with a couple of acres, and a church full of crazies down the bend. The women yelling and rolling, Carmody had laughed, fuck Jesus blind if they could, and Parson thought, in the jostle and roar of the truck cab, of Jesus, the mystery, taking a woman to him as Preacher had taken women, sometimes in Parson's little room, on Parson's cot, pious women feverish with guilt or want. Preacher was a big man, heavy, clothed in black and the dark woollen coat he wore in winters; beneath him the women seemed prostrate as he worked over them, performing a sacrament that elicited the heaving breath of hard labour. Sent out for wood, Parson watched from the window at the foot of the bed, seeing only Preacher's backside and the woman's white legs straddling the edges of the narrow cot or flung up over Preacher's behind. He was too big to hold in his bulky clothes and their flimsy, imploring limbs were useless. Parson could see nothing, really, the women saw nothing, it was fast and hard and he got inside them without taking off their clothes, without removing his own, then he sat up over them, still panting, pulled them upright and prayed over them. It wasn't the young girls who came around but the older women, thin ones dried and wan like something had left them too long in the sun. Left for dead, Preacher would say, and they never told, only never came back or returned when they couldn't stay away. They needed that punishing comfort, the sharp heat of it, Preacher said, and he was a grievous sinner tempted by need, a sinner as surely as any murderer or thief, he brought sinners to the Crucible because he was a sinner himself. He trusted only the big women, women like Carmody's wife, he said they slept in their bodies, had vanquished the Devil in the fortification of the flesh. They were the ones to whom he delegated the organization of church suppers and revivals, the posting of notices. They brought food to the back porch in baskets, breads and cakes and roasted meats, home-made butter faded and white as the worn complexions of those other women, who stumbled through the door of Parson's low-ceilinged room as though they were faint or sick, who flung themselves down on the narrow cot in the sway of an urge Parson felt, watching them. Like a fire in his guts, sick with burning, and when he told Preacher the old man said he must spill his seed on barren ground, never in the house or in his bed, seduced by pleasure, he must cleanse himself kneeling and alone where the earth was hard, or in the cold of the river. *Throw it in the river*, Preacher said, that is the seed of evil, a weapon against the purity of God. Too late for a man of sixty, but Parson might remain clean. He was a big boy, Preacher said, an animal needy as a dog or a horse, a man never mothered by a woman, but he must pour the passion of the body into the work of the Lord, and Parson began to lead prayers at meetings, and to preach. He spoke of evil, having known it, he spoke of smelling its approach and described the smell, he spoke of the Devil's fragrant oils and the swollen itch of the Devil's hunger, of staunching the flow of the Devil's bloody need for that need was a mortal wound in the temple of the Lord, a bloody wound at the breast of Jesus, who took no woman and no man and was loved by God. Yet the Devil cleaved unto whatever fed him and feasted, drunk with flesh, feasted until he failed to defend his mind from angels. It was then Parson felt himself empowered as a warrior of the Lord, free to suck at the marrow of the Devil's enfeebled bones. Sitting in the cab of yet another truck on that journey to Greenbriar, he'd seen the familiar valleys and hovering brackish mountains, the small encroachable skies of southern West Virginia. The land revealed itself like an old dream as the trucker turned on a gospel station and radio chants of songs Parson had led in prison services broke over him like benedictions. Yes, he'd been right to follow Carmody, whose scared maniacal anger so readily changed, turned to a lax and satiated evil those nights he traded his wife's mailed parcels of clothes and food to the guards for liquor. Then he ranted about girls and women, crouching beside Parson's bunk to rasp in coarse whispers how he'd battered this one or that one with a cock like a wood plank till she screamed and begged for more, then he'd whipped her around and shoved it up before she could pull away, ha, they never wanted to do that, up the behind where it was good and tight, Parson knew, sure, reform school boy, foster kid, how they paid attention when you turned them over and piled in, had to hold on and shove till your lights came on and then they couldn't get loose to crawl away, eh? right? better do me, this is your chance, till Parson grabbed him to shut him up, to stop his evil mouth, the cell glowing blue with the Devil's light in the blackout of prison black, like being inside a grave, and Parson punched him on to the floor in the corner and held him down, and he felt silken, tasted sweet, as though his body retained some childish perfume despite the loutish, feline sneak in the man. But the flesh of the Devil seduced and fondled was always sweet, not

foul with the stench of death like the Devil betrayed and
wandering. Carmody groaned and arched himself and fondled his
hands into Parson's thick, dark hair, trying to push that wet
mouth lower, harder, and Parson heard the Devil's suckling cries,
the Devil's whimpering want, and he raised up to lie full length
upon the Devil's form. He balanced himself there and felt his
hands at the throat of the Demon, squeezing the sound and the
taste, and Carmody began to buck like a horse. Parson released
him then, sat up and hit him once, hard in the face, and left him
there, motionless, crawled on to his own bunk, arranging his
limbs as one would arrange articles on a shelf. He often felt his
body to be an object, something to be moved here and there, and
he felt most free when he had seen the Devil in some vulnerable
guise and subdued him, beat him back with a power he watched
himself employ. The power was a mystery, sudden, unquestioned,
overwhelming, full of air and wind, like flying, rising up in the air
clothed in raiment, clean and glowing. All during the trip to
Greenbriar Camp Parson had felt some remnant of that power
just clinging to the edges of his vision, a fuzz along the plane of
the highway, a vibration of colour where the landscape met the
sky. He'd got as far as Gaither and walked out Route 19, past
the Prison Labour buildings and the chair factory, and a
construction crew in a pick-up stopped to give him a ride. They
worked at the camp, laying pipe, and said they might use him if
he wanted to sign on. Slow work, and hot, digging and hauling,
but they hoped to make it last all summer and they could pay
him under the table, cash, no stubs or checks. Parson agreed. The
Lord continued to provide, just as he'd provided Pruntytown and
the meeting with Preacher, and the long road, even earlier, of
foster keepers tainted with evil, some of the evil seductive and
sweet. Then prison after Preacher died, prison a concentration of
evil and grace, like being sealed in a concrete tomb, a cave or
catacomb, Parson an ancient prophet, alone seven years with
only the voice of the Lord. The Lord God had rolled away the
rock as surely as for his holy Son, and Parson had walked to a
deliverance meant for him, for Carmody, for this place, the camp
in the trees. Riding all night in the trucks of mercy on spotlit
roads, he'd almost forgotten the world, but the world rushed him

fast as fever that morning—close faces of the workmen, beer bottle open on the dash, day heating up and the dense overhanging trees unstirred. He'd gone with them to the camp, they'd given him worn khaki work shirts and trousers, and he'd worked all day for an advance on his week's wages, given him that evening at a roadhouse where they all had hamburgers and beer. He was passing through, Parson told them, but he reckoned he was meant to work with them awhile. He told stories he'd heard other inmates tell, about working construction in Houston by the canal, how the wetbacks would fall asleep at night in the irrigation ditch and drown when the canal was flushed. Then they were straight and dead as logs. Parson had never really seen Houston but he thought at night, alone, of how the bodies looked, floating, buoyed by every motion of the water. He saw the water dark and full like ink, like the black dark in the shack at night, the forest and the camp crouched nearby, breathing. He could float like death in this darkness, awake and nearly dreaming. And when he rose in one effortless movement to look out the window at Turtle Hole, he felt he had moved merely by imagining movement. The water shone and the black boulder overhanging one side was darker than the air around it. The boy, Frank, sat fishing, suspended in the dark like an ornament. His bare chest looked unnaturally white, and when he threw his line out Parson could feel the hook rip through resisting water. The boy was up late tonight. Parson imagined him drowsy and bored, a high school kid too young to drive, passing time in a summer job that left him free to do as he liked after chores. Mornings at seven, he blew reveille on a beat-up trumpet at the quad, hauled this or that for Carmody's big wife, there to cook breakfast by six. He played the national anthem at flag raising, just before all the girls trooped inside to long tables, then he went around back to eat in the kitchen. The workmen down by the river could hear him on the trumpet, the sound was so piercing, warbling and breaking on the high notes, and behind his song the girls' voices were faint and dreamy as the voices of sleepwalkers. Parson had never seen them, saluting in a circular line; the men were already at work by then, or at least gathered by the river to drink coffee. Three of them brought tall thermoses and the rest drank from plastic cups while the foreman laid plans, but the plans were always the same—dig out earth for ten foot of pipe, lay the pipe, and spend afternoon cutting brush for a trail road for the truck. They kept the trail close but wound around stands of trees too near the riverbank; sometimes they dragged pipe with chains as far as thirty, forty feet, in teams, like horses. Sweating, cursing the whole Mickey Mouse operation, they paced themselves with their own insolent complaints while the foreman cursed loudest how he'd only taken the job because the mines had laid him off. Occasionally the little girls appeared, hiking the forested hills across the river in crooked lines. They were led by college girl counsellors and their faces appeared and disappeared amongst the trees, their white blouses forming a shifting, patchy mosaic. Sprites, the men called them, as though they were forest spirits, and when they were too high up or far away to see, their laughter and their urgent, childish speech carried down bright and tiny, perfectly preserved. The older girls, camping higher in the hills and never seen, were subjects of speculation and offhand jokes only because the camp directoress had asked the men not to set foot across the river without special permission. They were discouraged from walking through the camp except when they were on their way to or from the work site, as though Girl Guides were somehow threatened by the vision of five men in khakis. They'd said as much to Frank, who was sent out hot afternoons with paper cups and a big jug of cold lemonade, and Frank told them he didn't work for Mrs Thompson-Warner and Hilda Carmody didn't either, or they wouldn't be getting any lemonade. The place was just rented out to Girl Guides these three weeks, then there was a church camp coming and the Y-Teens, and the camp was vacant part of August. Probably it would shut down. Figure I could hire on with you men? But the foreman had smiled, his lips wet with the cold sweetened liquid. Boy can't do a man's job, you a boy, ain't you? I can dig, he'd said, and I got my own tent I stay in. I don't think so, kid, but you tell that fat woman she makes good lemonade. Sweet as a baby's tits. Those women you take orders from know how much time you spend spying on the girls up at the top of the hill? I don't go up there, the boy had said, they gotta do everything themselves. And the foreman had joked about *everything*, how that old red-headed dame sure seemed worried about those girls, worried about somebody. Nah, she's worried about Communists, Frank had said. Yes, she was worried. At night in the shack Parson could feel her worry in her sleep, her powdered forehead creased while the Devil passed in and out her open window. Those white frilly curtains she'd hung rippled each time the Devil moved, and his legs were the flayed red colour of raw meat, and wet like that, and the smell in her room was the smell of blood. Some nights Parson walked about at night, and he'd seen those sheer curtains fluttering, blown out ghostly and helpless. He could see them from far off, at her window in the back of the dining-hall, after he crossed the quad off the trail that came in from the river. He only wandered where he chose at night, circling Turtle Hole, hearing the river through the trees and following the quiet silver flat of it around the base of the camp. Days he was careful, leaving with the other men and circling back behind the border of the woods after supper at a roadhouse two miles off. The roadhouse smelled of fly paper, of salty dust and men's sweat. The directoress smelled of vanilla, like a cake—some perfume she wore—and she was white as cake and soft and round, and she was no mate for the Demon. But she scared Parson because the Demon would work through her to get to someone else, many others maybe, she'd be no prize for the Devil, no barrier to His greed, but the Devil was near her like a shadow. She knew about evil, she was afraid, and she'd spoken the Devil's names. She'd sent for Parson, for anyone in the work crew, to drive the camp truck to the dump, and Parson went around to the back of the hall after work. Frank had piled up the junk and the directoress stood waiting while Parson took the keys and backed the truck around. He got out to load up and she pointed to the cover of a magazine, top one in a pile tied with twine. There is Lucifer in the flesh, there is Beelzebub, there is the Devil himself, she'd said. Parson looked at her and felt she was somehow kin to the big, lonely women in Preacher's congregations, women who had fanned themselves while Parson spoke of evil and retribution. But this one was wealthy, she held herself drawn up and tense, she wanted to be clean, like fine white cake. The Devil takes many forms, Parson told her. She'd pointed to the magazine and the image of a short, fat bald man whose hairless face seemed swollen, whose tiny, bright eyes were squeezed small like a pig's. The Democrats are fools to think of a treaty with Khrushchev, she went on while Parson loaded junk, boxes of empty metal cans, broken lengths of wood, spotted linoleum flooring ripped up in irregular pieces. He smelled her sugary smell, like a bake shop, a smell suddenly so specific that he felt dizzy, remembering the hotel sweet shop down in Greensboro where Preacher had played cards. They'd gone to a revival down in Carolina and Preacher got wind of a high-stakes game. The hotel was fancy, the sweet shop all pink and white. There were swans made of sweet crust filled with yellow cream, their long necks dipped in chocolate. People have to be educated to recognize evil, the directoress said, voice at his back, then, Better load that refrigerator now or you won't have room. Straining to lift the empty doorless cabinet Parson shut out the sound of her and recited a litany of his own, a litany so fast he never had to speak, just move his lips, sounds meant to shut out the sugar and the sweets and the images of that night in Greensboro when Preacher had got shot. Parson remembered pieces of it, like the sweet shop where they'd stood before walking upstairs to the room. The long glass cases held trays of pastry swans in lines, and cookies in the shapes of four-leaf clovers, sprinkled with sugar bits. The sugar was green as bottle glass, glinting in minute squares. St Pat's Day, it had been, a day for pagans, but it was snowing that late in March, a freak storm. The hotel had been warm, and the sugar smell was heady. Parson was eighteen and he had never seen . . . a sugar swan. Peering in at eye level, he saw a flotilla of confections on paper lace, their wings and necks moulded dark with chocolate. So perfect, made for no reason or use. What sort of children held these sweets in their palms, even ate them as though they were bread or meat? Children far from the smell of the wind in Calvary, the river blown smell of wet growth, algae, the greeny water where frogs bred after the thaw, their eggs a fresh rot smell somehow kin to the sour yogurt smell of women. *The Devil has a beautiful face today*, Preacher had murmured, urging Parson away. They left the sweet shop and the long stairs upwards were dark oiled wood, and the walls were dark wood ascending upwards into darkness. Parson remembered the upstairs bedroom where the men had gambled, smoke in the air, a shirt flung over the lamp so the light was dim. There were lines of talk he remembered, *should have seen him, big grown kid wants a sugar sweet*, and how one of the men had sent down for a tray of the pastries but Parson wouldn't eat one, only held it in his hand, looking, and later during the fight the whole tray of them was thrown into the fire, the bitter smell of the burnt sugar pungent as the smell of burning hair. The fire had crackled, exploded, or the explosion was in the room, and the table had gone over, cards in the air a slow arc that rained on Parson's face. Then another crack, loud, like lightning, and the other men were gone, out the window to the metal fire escape stairs, nearly falling in a jumble, their arms and legs jerking like sticks as they descended, growing smaller against the snow. The smell of human guts was like the smell in the den of a beast, and evil had filled the room, smoky, darkening all but the comets that flashed as Parson rolled Preacher on to his back like a black-sacked bag of feed. Preacher's front was slick with an oil that splashed red on the floor, on the window, on the snow that coated the metal fire escape and out there in the air the day was blinding white, whiter and whiter. The directoress's powdered face was not even so white when she put her face close to Parson and said, Well, get along now, that's all there is. He stepped away from her because he saw the Devil leering from behind in his shadow dress, a thin wraith of a Devil in a shadow cloak as wide as this woman, then the Devil was a grey wrinkle at her side, fading off completely. Where do you live, the directoress asked, and Parson told her he stayed with his brother, Carmody, in a house down the road. You mean Hilda's family, Hilda, the cook? Yes, Carmody, Parson said, for he was with Carmody, always near him, breathing his look and his smell, watching his big wife arrive every morning at Greenbriar Camp with the blond kid in tow, pulling the kid across the quad like a weightless paper toy on a string. He could almost imagine the inside of Carmody's wooden house and the dirt flat of the backyard, or was it grassy and overgrown, sloping off to the narrow stream that fed the river and rattled through the woods? I'll bring the truck right back, he'd told the directoress, and suddenly she straightened, looked him in the eye and held out her hand. I'm Virginia Thompson-Warner, regional secretary of the Daughters of the American Revolution. I certainly respect your sister-in-law, she accomplishes a great deal almost single-handedly. She touched Parson, grasping him, and her hand in his was flat and thick and cool as the raw white breast of a fish. Parson nodded, pulling away, feeling in her fingers an echo of the blue shade that fell across the woods just after sunset, when the illumined green of foliage spotlit by an angled descent of light suddenly gave way. The woods were unlit, cast in a warm, still pall those moments before evening began, commenced in a chorus of insect sound. Later, in the shack at night, Parson could hear the lost blue shade of the sudden summer dusks still wandering, hear it in the flights of the scavenger creatures, the owls and bats, and finally the dusk gathered like cool smoke over Turtle Hole. Preacher was not there in the smoke, it was so cool and blue, but Parson felt him in the shack itself. He never appeared as some of the others, doomed or dead, appeared, he was present and vanished just as he'd vanished that day in the room, gone even as Parson staggered under his weight on the slippery metal stairs of the fire escape. Snow turned to rain over all the grey parking lot behind the hotel as Parson dragged them both to Preacher's old pick-up, going through the old man's pockets for the keys as he held the falling bulk of his burden up against the cab of the truck. Preacher was still breathing, a sound like rasps of air through ragged holes, and Parson got him into the truck, his own hands and front bloodied, pulling fast out of the lot as the attendant came to the door of the little booth. Parson didn't think of hospitals, he thought only of getting away, going home, Preacher would want to go home. He had driven several streets, roaring down alleys to cut out towards the highway, trying to hold Preacher upright with one arm, when the girl's startled face and form appeared like an apparition beyond the wet glass of the windshield. There was the dull thud of contact overwhelmed by the scream of the brakes and the girl flew up on to the broad hood of the truck, rolling hard, coming for Parson, flying as though impelled into the windshield, hitting lengthwise across it head to foot, assaulting Parson with her wet yellow hair and wide death gaze. She was like a fish with thin human arms outspread, a fish in

a flimsy raincoat with a girl's blue face, slapping so hard on the
wet glass that Parson screamed into her broken shape, screamed
even after she rolled back along the hood and on to the street. In
the shack at night he remembered the trundling sound her body
had made rolling away, an object out of its element, because she
was a fish, that was clear when the police came and he stood
looking down at her in the wet street. This man is shot to death,
they'd said about Preacher, and grabbed Parson's arms as though
he might run, but they had to drag him away. He only wanted to
look at her, this fish, the ends of her long yellow hair spiky with
moisture, her wet coat open, her limbs pulled close as though she
were one long shape and might ripple across the puddled surface
of the pavement like an eel. But they covered her and put him in a
squad car and he didn't see her again until he got to the
penitentiary in Carolina nearly six months later, and she would
swim at night, naked, thin and white, through the darkened main
corridor of the cell block. The dark there was green and oily,
nearly phosphorescent, and she swam face forward, her wet hair
flat to her head, legless, armless, her body one undulating streak.
This night when he woke in the shack, Parson saw Frank fishing
Turtle Hole, the long bamboo pole barely visible over the water.
He imagined the girl who was a fish, circling deep within the bowl
of water, down where the line and hook would never touch. The
boy seemed to hang suspended against the dark rock, pulling his
line out of the water again and again only to throw it across to the
same spot, raking the surface in slow swaths. He seemed to break
the water gingerly, stirring it in careful identical sweeps as though
it were volatile. But the water slept. Parson saw the two girls long
before Frank knew they were there, he saw them edging across the
river trail from the woods, moving carefully and quickly, nearly in
tandem. They were not ghosts. One was in white but for her dark
pants. The other was more than human. Nude, whiter still, she
followed the first as though to restate each gesture and step with
longer, thinner limbs, a long bound shimmer of pale hair moving
behind her. They had no faces, only forms, and the paler, more
fluid one swam the air as though walking. Parson went to the door
of the shack and beyond it, moving soundlessly closer, crouching
along the barely discernible trail to the water. No, she was

different, but she was the same, as if she were sister to the one in the street, the one who might swim still in some dark space, searching for him. And would never find him, never, until he was a shade himself. Already he saw and heard as a shade, hearing no voices now but feeling himself inside the mind of the girl who might be a fish, himself surrounded by a magnified, sonorous pulse and a great ruffling of air. She might be capable of flight, there was such wind in her, and electric blue flares that shot up like fires, and in the dark of her something cracked, loud as the crack of a gun, kept cracking apart. He shook himself to be outside her again, watching, and in a moment he saw them, on their knees in the reeds at the edge of Turtle Hole. Frank had not seen them, he must be nearly sleeping, staring at the unbroken surface of the water. The water was so still, as though enclosed in glass sheer as first ice. But the night air was warm, just cooling, and as Parson crept closer, so close he could see her face, the other girl stood, soundless, waiting for Frank to look at her. When he did, she knelt back into the reeds, and the taller one appeared, nearly opalescent above the dark grasses. She had a face like stone, stone shaped by hand: the brow, the wide-set eyes, the straight nose and parted lips. In jail in Greensboro, waiting to come to trial, he'd see from the high window two stone women tower above the court-house steps across the street. At night, the streets deserted, the building lit so their shadows fell across the broad steps, Parson imagined the end of the world, no people at all but just these buildings, sidewalks, long empty streets, and the statues fallen over. Now he imagined this girl as one of them, the whole white length of her lying not in the depths of Turtle Hole but in the stream, which was shallow and looked so clear, her face washed by water until the regular features and cast of eye were obscured. Until she was smooth as scooped stone, long and tapered in her body, a rock fish, a fish with breasts. Her breasts were like white apples, full and compact, young, not the large breasts men slept in, but breasts men mouthed and tasted, nearly tore with their teeth. The nipples were like faint bruises at the centres. Parson saw Frank, unmoving on the rock like an animal light blinded, and knew he was so startled at the appearance of her body that he had not really seen her face. He looked, kept

197

looking, and as he did she lifted each foot gently, never altering her gaze, so the other girl could remove her shoes. Then she walked into the water as though drawn to its centre, as though she would walk until she disappeared, and the boy stood and jumped in. *I threw it in the water*, Parson had told the men in Carolina. They were men in suits but there were no windows in the little room, they took off their jackets and rolled up their sleeves. There was the one who gave Parson cigarettes and called him 'son', and the one who shoved Parson from wall to wall while the light swung on its cord overhead. Parson remembered the heat and how the men had paced like big hot dogs who could only sweat from their tongues. Who shot him? Who were the other men? Did you shoot him? Where's the gun the gun the gun—They had come straight for him in the fluid, moving room just as the boy swam for her now, and Parson watched her lift herself, hold to Frank's shoulders as though she might drink the whole deep bowl of Turtle Hole, drown as Parson had drowned in the cage room that smelled of those men. The girl was a fish, he'd told them, lost from Christ, they were lost, Preacher had gambled on evil, and the room had circled as the whole sheen of Turtle Hole now began to circle, stirred to move by their bodies and the silence they made until the other girl waded in, her clothes wet and darkened, her darker hair a black cap. She was the dark one who put her mouth on them, touched them, she and Frank held her between them until she cried out and the sound she kept making froze Parson's blood, he had to lie down in the reeds and hold himself tight, clutch his ears, but she went on and he began to try to crawl away, move backwards like an animal in a narrow space. This is how that other one would have sounded had she opened her mouth and let a sound roll from her long white throat. In all the years he had seen her, navigating dark air like a sea, she had not made this sound from death. The sound went on like mourning, eating its own fear, released and saved, and when it stopped Parson could not remember where he was, all of space seemed so empty. But it was night in Greenbriar Camp and the girls moved in the silver water, emerged pouring water from their bodies, the naked one shining, stumbling, and they ran then, gained the path and were gone. Parson watched Frank, who called once to them and followed, just to the edge of the water. The boy lay down then, wanted to sleep but roused himself, walked back through the woods to where Parson knew he had a tent in a clearing near the cave. Now the night looked blue. There was silence but for a far-off wind just grazing the woods by the river, and the rustling of those leaves was half-heard. The moon would lighten the air even more and in an hour, two hours, mist would settle above the water, never touching, so that the surface could still be seen and the white smoky vapour might be hung above it from invisible cords. Parson walked to where the girls had stood and saw that they had left the shoes. He took them to the shack and felt them all over, looked at them in the glint of the window, then remembered the flashlight one of the workmen had given him. He took it from under the corner of his pallet and shone the short, wide beam of its light across the shoes. They were white canvas sneakers with frayed shoe-strings. One of them had a cloth decal of Mickey Mouse (Parson remembered the foreman had said *a Mickey Mouse operation*) sewn inside. The other had a gummed label on which was written: LENNY.

BRITISH BLOOD

CUTTING EDGE

John Harvey £13.99

Charlie Resnick - hero of LONELY HEARTS and ROUGH TREATMENT - investigates a series of seemingly motiveless assaults on workers at a large teaching hospital.

Past praise:

"British crime fiction coming of age."   The Face

A GERMAN REQUIEM

Philip Kerr £13.99

Bernie Gunther leaves the post-war Berlin of MARCH VIOLETS and THE PALE CRIMINAL for Vienna, to check up on ex-KRIPO colleague turned black-marketeer Emil Becker.

Past praise:

"A sound sense of history; powerful period flavour; a gruff, subversive hero. Kerr delivers the goods."
Literary Review

BAD TO THE BONE

Brian Thompson £13.99

An impressive crime debut by the award-winning novelist and screenwriter. A gripping thriller of greed and betrayal cutting through the social layers of contemporary Britain.

VIKING

NADINE GORDIMER
SOME ARE BORN TO SWEET DELIGHT
TO SWEET DELIGHT

Nadine Gordimer

Some are born to sweet delight
Some are born to endless night
William Blake, 'Auguries of Innocence'

They took him in. Since their son had got himself signed up at sea for eighteen months on an oil rig, the boy's cubbyhole of a room was vacant; and the rent money was a help. There had rubbed off on the commissionaire's braid on the father's uniform, through the contact of club members' coats and brief-cases he relieved them of, loyal consciousness of the danger of bombs affixed under the cars of Members of Parliament and financiers. The father said 'I've no quarrel with that,' when the owners of the house whose basement flat the family occupied stipulated 'No Irish'. But to discriminate against any other foreigners from the old Empire was against the principles of the house owners, who were also the mother's employers—cleaning three times a week and baby-sitting through the childhood of three boys she thought of as her own. So it was a way of pleasing Upstairs to let the room to this young man, a foreigner who likely had been turned away from other vacancies posted on a board at the supermarket. He was clean and tidy enough; and he didn't hang around the kitchen, hoping to be asked to eat with the family, the way one of their own kind would. He didn't eye Vera.

Vera was seventeen, and a filing clerk with prospects of advancement; her father had got her started in an important firm through the kindness of one of his gentlemen at the club. A word in the right place; and now it was up to her to become a secretary, maybe one day even a private secretary to someone like the members of the club, and travel to the Continent, America—anywhere.

—You have to dress decently for a firm like that. Let others show their backsides.—

—Dad!—The flat was small, the walls thin: suppose the lodger heard him. Her pupils dilated with a blush, half shyness, half annoyance. On Friday and Saturday nights she wore T-shirts with spangled graffiti across her breasts and went with girl-friends to the discothèque, although she'd had to let the pink side of her hair grow out. On Sundays they sat on wooden benches outside the pub with teasing local boys, drinking beer shandies. Once it was straight beer laced with something and they made her drunk, but her father had been engaged as doorman for a private party and her mother had taken the Upstairs children to the zoo, so nobody heard her vomiting in the bathroom.

So she thought.

He was in the kitchen when she went, wiping the slime from her panting mouth, to drink water. He always addressed her as 'miss'—Good afternoon, miss.—He was himself filling a glass.

She stopped where she was; sourness was in her mouth and nose, oozing towards the foreign stranger, she mustn't go a step nearer. Shame tingled over nausea and tears. Shame heaved in her stomach, her throat opened and she just reached the sink in time to disgorge the final remains of a pizza minced by her teeth and digestive juices, floating in beer.—Go away. Go away!—her hand flung in rejection behind her. She opened both taps to blast her shame down the drain.—Get out!—

He was there beside her, in the disgusting stink of her, and he had wetted a dish-towel and was wiping her face, her dirty mouth, her tears. He was steadying her by the arm and sitting her down at the kitchen table. And she knew that his kind didn't even drink, he probably never had smelled alcohol before. If it had been one of her own crowd it would have been different.

She began to cry again. Very quietly, slowly, he put his hand on hers, taking charge of the wrist like a doctor preparing to follow the measure of a heart in a pulse-beat. Slowly—the pace was his—she quietened; she looked down, without moving her head, at the hand. Slowly, she drew her own hand from underneath, in parting.

As she left the kitchen a few meaningless echoes of what had happened to her went back and forth—are you all right yes I'm all right are you sure yes I'm all right.

She slept through her parents' return and next morning said she'd had flu.

He could no longer be an unnoticed presence in the house, outside her occupation with her work and the friends she made among the other junior employees, and her preoccupation, in her leisure, with the discothèque and cinema where the hand-holding and sex-tussles with local boys took place. He said—Good afternoon—as they saw each other approaching in the passage between the family's quarters and his room, or couldn't avoid coinciding at the gate of the tiny area garden where her mother's geraniums bloomed and the empty milk bottles were set out. He didn't say 'miss'; it was as if the omission were saying—Don't worry, I won't tell anyone, *although I know all about what you do*, everything, I won't talk about you among my friends—did he even have any friends? Her mother told her he worked in the kitchens of a smart restaurant—her mother had to be sure a lodger had steady pay before he could be let into the house. Vera saw other foreigners like him about, gathered loosely as if they didn't know where to go; of course, they didn't come to the disco and they were not part of the crowd of familiars at the cinema. They were together but looked alone. It was something noticed the way she might notice, without expecting to fathom, the strange expression of a caged animal, far from wherever it belonged.

She owed him a signal in return for his trustworthiness. Next time they happened to meet in the house she said—I'm Vera.—

As if he didn't know, hadn't heard her mother and father call her. Again he did the right thing, merely nodded politely.

—I've never really caught your name.—

—Our names are hard for you, here. Just call me Rad.—His English was stiff, pronounced syllable by syllable in a soft voice.

—So it's short for something?—

—What is that?—

—A nickname. Bob for Robert.—

—Something like that.—

She ended this first meeting on a new footing the only way she knew how: —Well, see you later, then—the vague dismissal used casually among her friends when no such commitment existed. But on a Sunday when she was leaving the house to wander down to see who was gathered at the pub she went up the basement steps and saw that he was in the area garden. He was reading newspapers—three or four of them lying on the mud-plastered grass at his side. She picked up his name and used it for the first time, easily as a key turning in a greased lock.—Hullo, Rad.—

He rose from the chair he had brought out from his room. —I hope your mother won't mind? I wanted to ask, but she's not at home.—

—Oh no, not Ma, we've had that old chair for ages, a bit of fresh air won't crack it up more than it is already.—

She stood on the short path, he stood beside the old rattan chair; then sat down again so that she could walk off without giving offence—she left to her friends, he left to his reading.

She said—I won't tell.—

And so it was out, what was between them alone, in the family house. And they laughed, smiled, both of them. She walked over to where he sat.—Got the day off? You work in a restaurant, don't you, what's it like?—

—I'm on the evening shift today.—He stayed himself a moment, head on one side, with aloof boredom.—It's something. Just a job. What you can get.—

—I know. But I suppose working in a restaurant at least the food's thrown in, as well.—

He looked out over the railings a moment, away from her. —I don't eat that food.—

She began to be overcome by a strong reluctance to go through the gate, round the corner, down the road to The Mitre and the whistles and appreciative pinches which would greet her in her new flowered Bermudas, his black eyes following her all the way, although he'd be reading his papers with her forgotten. To gain time she looked at the papers. The one in his hand was English. On the others, lying there, she was confronted with a flowing script of tails and gliding flourishes, the secret of somebody else's language. She could not go to the pub; she could not let him know that was where she was going. The deceptions that did for parents were not for him. But the fact was there was no deception: she *wasn't* going to the pub, she suddenly wasn't going.

She sat down on the motoring section of the English newspaper he'd discarded and crossed her legs in an X from the bare round knees.—Good news from home?—

He gestured with his foot towards the papers in his secret language; his naked foot was an intimate object, another secret.

—From my home, no good news.—

She understood this must be some business about politics over there: she was in awe and ignorance of politics, nothing to do with her.—So that's why you went away.—

He didn't need to answer.

—You know, I can't imagine going away.—

—You don't want to leave your friends.—

She caught the allusion, pulled a childish face, dismissing them.—Mum and Dad . . . everything.—

He nodded, as if in sympathy for her imagined loss but made no admission of what must be his own.

—Though I'm mad keen to travel. I mean, that's my idea, taking this job. Seeing other places, just visiting, you know. If I make myself capable and that, I might get the chance. There's one secretary in our offices who goes everywhere with her boss, she brings us all back souvenirs, she's very generous.—

—You want to see the world. But now your friends are waiting for you.—

She shook off the insistence with a laugh.—And you want to go home!—

—No.—He looked at her with the distant expression of an adult before the innocence of a child.—Not yet.—

The authority of his mood over hers, that had been established in the kitchen that time, was there. She was hesitant and humble rather than flirtatious when she changed the subject.

—Shall we have . . .will you have some tea if I make it? Is it all right?— He'd never eaten in the house; perhaps the family's food and drink were taboo for him in his religion, like the stuff he could have eaten free in the restaurant.

He smiled.—Yes it's all right.—And he got up and padded along behind her on his slim feet to the kitchen. As with a wipe over the clean surfaces of her mother's sink and table, the other time in the kitchen was cleared by ordinary business about brewing tea, putting out cups. She set him to cut the gingerbread:

—Go on, try it, it's my mother's home-made.—She watched with an anxious smile, curiosity, while his beautiful teeth broke into its crumbling softness. He nodded, granting grave approval with a full mouth. She mimicked him, nodding and smiling; and, like a doe approaching a leaf, she took from his hand the fragrant slice with the semicircle marked by his teeth, and took a bite out of it.

Vera didn't go to the pub any more. At first they came to look for her—her chums, her mates—and nobody believed her excuses when she wouldn't come along with them. She hung about the house on Sundays, helping her mother.

—Have you had a tiff or something?—

As she always told her bosom friends, she was lucky with her kind of mother, not strict and suspicious like some.—No, Ma. They're OK, but it's always the same thing, same things to say, every weekend.—

—Well . . . shows you're growing up, moving on—it's natural. You'll find new friends, more interesting, more your type.—

Vera listened to hear if he was in his room or had had to go to work—his shifts at the restaurant, she had learnt from timing his presence and absences, were irregular. He was very quiet, didn't play a radio or cassettes but she always could feel if he was there, in his room. That summer was a real summer for once; if he was off shift he would bring the old rattan chair into the garden and read, or stretch out his legs and lie back with his face lifted to the humid sun. He must be thinking of where he came from; very hot, she imagined it, desert and thickly white cubes of houses with palm trees. She went out with a rug—nothing unusual about wanting to sunbathe in your own area garden —and chatted to him as if just because he happened to be there. She watched his eyes travelling from right to left along the scrolling print of his newspapers, and when he paused, yawned, rested his head and closed his lids against the light, could ask him about home—his home. He described streets and cities and cafés and bazaars—it wasn't at all like her idea of desert and oases.

—But there are palm trees?—

—Yes, night-clubs, rich people's palaces to show tourists, but there are also factories and prison camps and poor people living on a handful of beans a day.—

She picked at the grass: I see.—Were you—were your

family—do you like beans?—
He was not to be drawn; he was never to be drawn.
—If you know how to make them, they are good.—
—If we get some, will you tell us how they're cooked?—
—I'll make them for you.—
So one Sunday Vera told her mother Rad, the lodger, wanted to prepare a meal for the family. Her parents were rather touched; nice, here was a delicate mark of gratitude, such a glum character, he'd never shown any sign before. Her father was prepared to put up with something that probably wouldn't agree with him.—Different people, different ways. Maybe it's a custom with them, when they're taken in, like bringing a bunch of flowers.—The meal went off well. The dish was delicious and not too spicy; after all, gingerbread was spiced, too. When her father opened a bottle of beer and put it down at Rad's place, Vera quickly lifted it away.—He doesn't drink, Dad.—

Graciousness called forth graciousness; Vera's mother issued a reciprocal invitation.—You must come and have our Sunday dinner one day: my chicken with apple pie to follow.—

But the invitation was in the same code as 'See you later.' It was not mentioned again. One Sunday Vera shook the grass from her rug.—I'm going for a walk.—And the lodger slowly got up from his chair, put his newspaper aside, and they went through the gate. The neighbours must have seen her with him. The pair went where she led, although they were side by side, loosely, the way she'd seen young men of his kind together. They went on walking a long way, down streets and then into a park. She loved to watch people flying kites; now he was the one who watched her, watching. It seemed to be his way of getting to know her; to know anything. It wasn't the way of other boys—her kind—but then he was a foreigner here, there must be so much he needed to find out. Another weekend she had the idea to take a picnic. That meant an outing for the whole day. She packed apples and bread and cheese—remembering no ham—under the eyes of her mother. There was a silence between them. In it was her mother's recognition of the accusation she, Vera, knew she ought to bring against herself: Vera was 'chasing' a man; this man. All her mother said was—Are you joining other friends?—She didn't lie.

—No. He's never been up the river. I thought we'd take a boat trip.—

In time she began to miss the cinema. Without guile she asked him if he had seen this film or that; she presumed that when he was heard going out for the evening the cinema would be where he went, with friends of his—his kind—she never saw. What did they do if they didn't go to a movie? It wouldn't be bars, and she knew instinctively he wouldn't be found in a disco, she couldn't see him shaking and stomping under twitching coloured lights.

He hadn't seen any film she mentioned.—Won't you come?—It happened like the first walk.

He looked at her again as he had then.—D'you think so?—

—Why ever not? Everybody goes to the movies.—

But she knew why not. She sat beside him in the theatre with solemnity. It was unlike any other time, in that familiar place of pleasure. He did not hold her hand; only that time, that time in the kitchen. They went together to the cinema regularly. The silence between her and her parents grew; her mother was like a cheerful bird whose cage had been covered. Whatever her mother and father thought, whatever they feared—nothing had happened, nothing happened until one public holiday when Vera and the lodger were both off work and they went on one of their long walks into the country (that was all they could do, he didn't play sport, there wasn't any activity with other young people he knew how to enjoy). On that day celebrated for a royal birthday or religious anniversary that couldn't mean anything to him, in deep grass under profound trees he made love to Vera for the first time. He had never so much as kissed her before, not on any evening walking home from the cinema, not when they were alone in the house and the opportunity was obvious as the discretion of the kitchen clock sounding through the empty passage, and the blind eye of the television set in the sitting-room. All that he had never done with her was begun and accomplished with unstoppable passion, summoned up as if at a mere command to himself; between this and the placing of his hand on hers in the kitchen, months before, there was nothing. Now she had the lips from whom, like a doe, she had taken a

209

morsel touched with his saliva, she had the naked body promised by the first glimpse of the naked feet. She had lost her virginity, like all her sister schoolgirls, at fourteen or fifteen, she had been fucked, half-struggling, by some awkward local in a car or a back room, once or twice. But now she was overcome, amazed, engulfed by a sensuality she had no idea was inside her, a bounty of talent unexpected and unknown as a burst of song would have been welling from one who knew she had no voice. She wept with love for this man who might never, never have come to her, never have found her from so far away. She wept because she was so afraid it might so nearly never have happened. He wiped her tears, he dressed her with the comforting resignation to her emotion a mother shows with an over-excited child.

She didn't hope to conceal from her mother what they were doing; she knew her mother knew. Her mother felt her gliding silently from her room down the passage to the lodger's room, the room that still smelt of her brother, late at night, and returning very early in the morning. In the dark Vera knew every floorboard that creaked, how to avoid the swish of her pyjamas touching past a wall; at dawn she saw the squinting beam of the rising sun sloped through a window that she had never known was so placed it could let in any phase of the sun's passage across the sky. Everything was changed.

What could her mother have said? Maybe he had different words in his language; the only ones she and her mother had wouldn't do, weren't meant for a situation not provided for in their lives. *Do you know what you're doing? Do you know what he is? We don't have any objection to them, but all the same. What about your life? What about the good firm your father's got you into? What'll it look like, there?*

The innocent release of sensuality in the girl gave her an authority that prevailed in the house. She brought him to the table for meals, now; he ate what he could. Her parents knew this presence, in the code of their kind, only as the signal by which an 'engaged' daughter would bring home her intended. But outwardly between Vera and her father and mother the form was kept up that his position was still that of a lodger, a lodger who had somehow become part of the household in that capacity. There was no need for he himself to pretend or assume any role; he never showed any kind of presumption towards their daughter, spoke to her with the same reserve that he, a stranger, showed to them. When he and the girl rose from the table to go out together it was always as if he accompanied her, without interest, at her volition.

Because her father was a man, even if an old one and her father, he recognized the power of sensuality in a female and was defeated, intimidated by its obstinacy. *He* couldn't take the whole business up with her; her mother must do that. He quarrelled with his wife over it. So she confronted their daughter. *Where will it end?* Both she and the girl understood: he'll go back where he comes from, and where'll you be? He'll drop you when he's had enough of what he wanted from you.

Where would it end? Rad occasionally acknowledged her among his friends, now—it turned out he did have some friends, yes, young men like him, from his home. He and she encountered them in the street, and instead of excusing himself and leaving her waiting obediently like one of those pet dogs tied up outside the supermarket, as he usually had done when he went over to speak to his friends, he took her with him and, as if remembering her presence after a minute or two of talk, interrupted himself— She's Vera.—Their greetings, the way they looked at her, made her feel that he had told them about her, after all, and she was happy. They made remarks in their own language she was sure referred to her. If she had moved on, from the pub, the disco, the parents, she was accepted, belonged somewhere else.

And then she found she was pregnant. She had no girl-friend to turn to who could be trusted not to say those things: he'll go back where he comes from he'll drop you when he's had enough of what he wanted from you. After the second month she bought a kit from the pharmacy and tested her urine. Then she went to a doctor because that do-it-yourself thing might be mistaken.

—I thought you said you would be all right.—

That was all he said, after thinking for a moment, when she told him.

—Don't worry, I'll find something. I'll do something about

211

it. I'm sorry, Rad. Just forget it.—She was afraid he would stop loving her—her term for love-making. When she went to him tentatively that night he caressed her more beautifully and earnestly than ever while possessing her.

She remembered reading in some women's magazine that it was dangerous to do anything to get rid of 'it' (she gave her pregnancy no other identity) after three months. Through roundabout enquiries she found a doctor who did abortions, and booked an appointment, taking an advance on her holiday bonus to meet the fee asked.

—By the way, it'll be all over next Saturday. I've found someone.—Timidly she brought up the subject she had avoided between them.

He looked at her as if thinking very carefully before he spoke, thinking apart from her, in his own language, as she was often sure he was doing. Perhaps he had forgotten—it was really her business, her fault, she knew. Then he pronounced what neither had:—The baby?—

—Well . . .—She waited, granting this.

He did not take her in his arms, he did not touch her.—You will have the baby. We will marry.—

It flew from her awkward, unbelieving, aghast with joy: —You want to marry me!—

—Yes, you're going to be my wife.—

—Because of this: a baby?—

He was gazing at her intensely, wandering over the sight of her.—Because I've chosen you.—

Of course, being a foreigner, he didn't come out with things the way an English speaker would express them.

And I love *you*, she said, I love you, I love you—babbling through vows and tears. He put a hand on one of hers, as he had done in the kitchen of her mother's house; once, and never since.

She saw a couple in a mini-series standing hand-in-hand, telling them; 'We're getting married'—hugs and laughter. But she told her parents alone, without him there. It was safer that way, she thought, for him. And she phrased it in proof of his good intentions as a triumphant answer to her mother's warnings, spoken and unspoken.—Rad's going to marry me.—

—He wants to marry you?—Her mother corrected. The burst of a high-pitched cry. The father twitched an angry look at his wife.

Now it was time for the scene to conform to the TV family announcement.—We're going to get married.—

Her father's head flew up and sank slowly, he turned away.

—You want to be married to him?—Her mother's palm spread on her breast to cover the blow.

The girl was brimming feeling, reaching for them.

Her father was shaking his head like a sick dog.

—And I'm pregnant and he's glad.—

Her mother turned to her father but there was no help coming from him. She spoke impatiently flatly.—So that's it.—

—No, that's not it. It's not it at all.—She would not say to them 'I love him,' she would not let them spoil that by trying to make her feel ashamed.—It's what I want.—

—It's what she wants.—Her mother was addressing her father.

He had to speak. He gestured towards his daughter's body, where there was no sign yet to show life growing there.—Nothing to be done then.—

When the girl had left the room he glared at his wife.—Bloody bastard.—

—Hush. Hush.—There was a baby to be born, poor innocent.

And it was, indeed, the new life the father had gestured in Vera's belly that changed everything. The foreigner, the lodger—had to think of him now as the future son-in-law, Vera's intended—told Vera and her parents he was sending her to his home for his parents to meet her.

—To your country?—

He answered with the gravity with which, they realized, marriage was regarded where he came from.—The bride must meet the parents. They must know her as I know hers.—

If anyone had doubted the seriousness of his intentions—well, they could be ashamed of those doubts, now; he was sending her home, openly and proudly, his foreigner, to be accepted by his parents.—But have you told them about the baby, Rad?—She didn't express this embarrassment in front of her mother and father.—What do you think? That is why you are going.—He slowed, then spoke again.—It's a child of our family.—

So she was going to travel at last! In addition to every other joy! In a state of continual excitement between desire for Rad—now openly sharing her room with her—and the pride of telling her work-mates why she was taking her annual leave just then, she went out of her way to encounter former friends whom she had avoided. To say she was travelling to meet her fiancé's family; she was getting married in a few months, she was having a baby—yes—proof of this now in the rounding under the flowered jumpsuit she wore to show it off. For her mother, too, a son-in-law who was not one of their kind became a distinction rather than a shame.—Our Vera's a girl who's always known her own mind. It's a changing world, she's not one just to go on repeating the same life as we've had.—The only thing that hadn't changed in the world was joy over a little one coming. Vera was thrilled, they were all thrilled at the idea of a baby, a first grandchild. Oh that one was going to be spoilt all right! The prospective grandmother was knitting, although Vera laughed and said babies weren't dressed in that sort of thing any more, hers was going to wear those little unisex frogsuits in bright colours. There was a deposit down on a pram fit for an infant prince or princess.

It was understood that if the intended could afford to send his girl all the way home just to meet his parents before the wedding, he had advanced himself in the restaurant business, despite the disadvantages young men like him had in an unwelcoming country. Upstairs was pleased with the news; Upstairs came down one evening and brought a bottle of champagne as a gift to toast Vera, whom they'd known since she was a child, and her boy—much pleasant laughter when the prospective husband filled everyone's glass and then served himself with orange juice. Even the commissionaire felt confident enough to tell one of his gentlemen at the club that his daughter was getting married, but first about to go abroad to meet the young man's parents. His gentlemen's children were always travelling; in his ears every day were overheard snatches of destinations—'by bicycle in China, can you believe it' . . . 'two months in Peru, rather nice' . . . 'snorkelling on the Barrier Reef, last I heard.' *Visiting her future parents-in-law where there is desert and palm trees*; not bad.

The parents wanted to have a little party, before she left, a combined engagement party and farewell. Vera had in mind a few of her old friends brought together with those friends of his she'd been introduced to and with whom she knew he still spent some time—she didn't expect to go along with him, it wasn't their custom for women, and she couldn't understand their language, anyway. But he didn't seem to think a party would work. She had her holiday bonus (to remember what she had drawn it for, originally, was something, feeling the baby tapping its presence softly inside her, she couldn't believe of herself) and she kept asking him what she could buy as presents for his family—his parents, his sisters and brothers, she had asked and learned all their names. He said he would buy things, he knew what to get. As the day for her departure approached, he still had not done so.—But I want to pack! I want to know how much room to leave, Rad!—He brought some men's clothing she couldn't judge and some dresses and scarves she didn't like but didn't dare say so—she supposed the clothes his sisters liked were quite different from what she enjoyed wearing—a good thing she hadn't done the choosing.

She didn't want her mother to come to the airport; they'd both be too emotional. Leaving Rad was strangely different; it was not leaving Rad but going, carrying his baby, to the mystery that was Rad, that was in Rad's silences, his blind love-making, the way he watched her, thinking in his own language so that she could not follow anything in his eyes. It would all be revealed when she arrived where he came from. He had to work, the day she left, until it was time to take her to the airport. Two of his friends, whom she could scarcely recognize from the others in the group she had met occasionally, came with him to fetch her in the taxi one of them drove. She held Rad's hand, making a tight double fist on his thigh, while the men talked in their language. At the airport the others left him to go in alone with her. He gave her another, last-minute gift for home.—Oh Rad, where'm I going to put it? The ticket says one hand-baggage!—

But she squeezed his arm in happy recognition of his thoughts for his family.

—It can go in; easy, easy.—

He unzipped her carryall as they stood in the queue at the check-in counter. She knelt with her knees spread to accommodate her belly, and helped him.

—What is it, anyway? I hope not something that's going to break?—

He was making a bed for the package.—Just toys for my sister's kid. Plastic.—

—I could have put them in the suitcase; Oh Rad . . . what room'll I have for duty-free!—

In her excitement, she was addressing the queue for the American airline's flight which would take her on the first leg of her journey. These fellow passengers were another kind of foreigner, Americans, but she felt she knew them all; they were going to be travelling in her happiness, she was taking them with her.

She held him with all her strength and he kept her pressed against his body; she could not see his face. He stood and watched her as she went through passport control and she stopped again and again to wave but she saw Rad could not wave, could not wave. Only watch her until he could not see her any longer. And she saw him in her mind, still looking at her, as she had done at the beginning when she had imagined herself as still under his eyes if she had gone to the pub on a Sunday morning.

Over the sea, the airliner blew up in mid-air. Everyone on board died. The black box was recovered from the bed of the sea and revealed that there had been an explosion in the tourist-class cabin followed by a fire; and there the messages ended; silence, the disintegration of the plane. No one knows if all were killed outright or if some survived to drown. An inquiry into the disaster continued for a year. The background of every passenger was traced, and the circumstances that led to the journey of each. There were some arrests; people detained for questioning and then released. They were innocent—but they were foreigners, of course. Then there was another disaster of the same nature, and a statement from a group with an apocalyptic name representing a faction of the world's wronged, claiming the destruction of both planes in some complication of vengeance for holy wars, land annexation, invasions, imprisonments, cross-border raids, territorial disputes, bombings, sinkings, kidnappings no one outside the initiated could understand. A member of the group, a young man known as Rad among many other aliases, had placed in the hand-baggage of the daughter of the family with whom he lodged, and who was pregnant by him, an explosive device. Plastic. A bomb of a plastic type undetectable by the usual procedures of airport security.

Vera was chosen.

Vera had taken them all, taken her fellow passengers, taken the baby inside her down to endless night, along with her happiness.

PATRICK SÜSKIND
A MID-LIFE CRISIS

It was Thursday, 9 November 1989, at seven-fifteen p.m.—I was forty and two-thirds years old at the time—and I was in Paris, when I heard the bulletin on the French radio news; the East German government had decided to open the border between East and West from midnight that night.

Excellent, I thought. Things are moving at last. They're finally going to get the basic right to freedom of movement. At last even the GDR is falling into line with the shift towards reform, democracy and liberalization which Gorbachev had sketched out, and which had already been taken up by Hungary and Poland with Czechoslovakia and Bulgaria soon to follow. People even dared hope that Romania, suffering under the most repulsive of the Eastern potentates, might one day go the same way. I switched off the radio and went out to eat. At that stage the world was still in order. I still understood a bit about global politics. Swift though the pace of change in Europe was, it seemed nevertheless perfectly reasonable and predictable, and I was still able to follow it. I still felt more or less on top of events.

That was no longer true when, a few hours later, I returned from my meal. I don't remember whether it was before or after midnight—the ninth or the tenth, in other words—in any case, switching the radio on, this time to a German station, and arriving in the middle of a live broadcast from Berlin, where something akin to a carnival atmosphere seemed to have broken out, I heard an interview with the Mayor of Berlin, Walter Momper, culminating with him declaring: 'Tonight the people of Germany are the happiest people in the world.'

I was dumbstruck. I couldn't believe what I'd heard. I had to repeat the sentence aloud to myself: 'Tonight the people of Germany are the happiest people in the world.' I still couldn't understand it. Was the man off his head? Was he drunk? Was I? What did he mean, 'the people of Germany'? The citizens of the Federal Republic or of the GDR? The West or the East Berliners? All of them? Possibly even we Bavarians? Including perhaps myself? And how come 'happy'? Since when can a people—assuming for a moment that such a thing exists as *the German people*—since when can a people be happy? Am I supposed to be happy? And how can Walter Momper feel qualified to pronounce upon it?

Photo: Raymond Depardon (Magnum)

221

And I recalled the words of Gustav Heinemann, that most aloof and unshowy, and perhaps for that reason most typical of German presidents, who, when asked by a journalist whether he loved Germany, answered drily, 'I love my wife.'

Good God, Walter Momper, I thought, how could you have made such a gaffe! Tomorrow's editorials will ram your sentence down your throat. It will haunt you till the day you die. With just one phrase blurted out in the heat of the moment you've made yourself a laughing stock for all time!

But the next day, as I study the newspapers (there are no German ones left; they've been torn from the newsagents' hands) and listen eagerly to the radio, it seems that Walter Momper is the hero of the hour. Not only is no one forcing him to eat his words; on the contrary, his 'happiest people' phrase has become the motto of the moment and is later elevated (like 'Goal of the Month') to 'Phrase of the Month', and even 'Phrase of the Year, 1989'.

Hardly had I recovered from this shock when a few days later I came across the following quote in a newspaper from Willy Brandt, the hero of my youth and, like Momper, a Social Democrat: 'Let that which belongs together grow together.' It was impossible to avoid the conclusion that by this he meant the GDR and the Federal Republic, including all of Berlin.

Senility, I thought. Clearly a case of Alzheimer's, or some other age-related disturbance of reasoning and judgement. Just what exactly is it that belongs together, pray tell? Absolutely nothing! On the contrary: it is impossible to conceive of anything more dissimilar than the GDR and the Federal Republic! Different societies, different governments, different economic systems, different education systems, different living standards, different power block allegiances, different histories, different blood-alcohol limits—nothing will grow together because nothing belongs together. What a shame that Willy Brandt couldn't simply have withdrawn honourably from public life! Why did he have to stand up and peddle such nonsense, and risk his whole reputation in the process?

But once again I'd got it wrong. Just as Momper's phrase before, so Brandt's expression now became the saying of the day, enthusiastically applauded at mass meetings in East and West, taken up as a campaign slogan not only by his own party, but also by the parties of government, even by the Greens.

It was in this same context, albeit some time later, that my whole view of history and my entire political consciousness were to receive their third and final nasty surprise: it's February 1990 and I'm watching a German television report on Chancellor Kohl's return from Moscow where he had obtained (or thought he had obtained, it didn't make any difference in the end) Soviet agreement in principle to the question of German unity. Chancellor Kohl is standing in the central aisle of the aircraft, obviously in the best of moods, a full champagne glass in his hand which, so the reporter tells us, contains Crimean champagne, and he hollers down to the journalists and members of the delegation sitting at the back: 'Have you all got something to drink down there?' Aha, I think, it's the old boy's birthday and he's standing everyone a drink, how nice of him. Wrong by a mile! Chancellor Kohl's birthday, as I later find out from the encyclopaedia, is not until 3 April, and certainly not in February. And he's not simply buying a round because he just happens to be in such a good mood; no, assured by general murmurings of agreement that everyone does have something to drink, he raises his glass and cries: 'To Germany, then!' And the foreign minister, standing behind him and four-fifths obscured by him, moves a little to the side so that we can see him a little better, and he too raises his glass, somewhat more timidly perhaps, and drinks: 'To Germany!'

I was flabbergasted. To that day I had never seen a single person drink to Germany.

Now I have to admit that I don't set a great deal of store by drinking etiquette. The hearty proposing of toasts and, worse still, the slamming together of glasses that normally accompanies it has always seemed to me superfluous, embarrassing and a bit unhygenic. At most I might let slip a quiet 'Cheers!' and make a fleeting gesture of raising my glass. If it's absolutely necessary, and an unavoidably festive occasion demands it, then I might be prepared to drink to a person, an anniversary, or a graduation, perhaps even to such a nebulous entity as 'a happy future' or 'every success' or something similar—but never to a country. And of all the countries in the world, then least of all to Germany, with whose name—it's only fifty years ago!—the world war and Auschwitz are inextricably linked.

Yes, yes, I know, Chancellor Kohl didn't mean it that way when he drank 'to Germany'. It wasn't the old, aggressive Germany that he had in mind, but the Germany of the present and of the future, peaceful, civilized and bound to Europe. He was looking to the future, not to the past, of course I believe him . . .

It is just possible that I am more backward-looking, more sensitive in this area than he is, or maybe it's simply that I've had a different upbringing, one that prevents me, rightly or wrongly, from using certain words and phrases. Perhaps it really is the case that, as Rudolf Augstein, publisher of *Der Spiegel*, (who has recently been sounding like Kohl's journalistic batman) put it in an editorial: 'History in tune with Darwinism manifestly does not allow enough time for the backward look, for the business of mourning so beneficial to mankind.' Maybe not. I myself am certainly not in tune with Darwinism; I like to leave myself enough time to look backwards, or forwards, or upwards, and when I hear a toast like Chancellor Kohl's then I have the distinct feeling that history in tune with Darwinism has, with one giant step, just passed me by. I lose the beat.

At around the same time as Chancellor Kohl was proposing his toast, his opponent in the race for the premiership, Oscar Lafontaine, was making a speech at an SPD rally in which he said that the question of German unity seemed to him a problem of the second rank: he thought it much more important to ensure that people in Leipzig, Dresden and East Berlin would be as well provided for as people in Vienna, Frankfurt, Paris or Madrid. I pricked up my ears. At last, after so many unintelligible words, a sentence that I understood. Quite apart from whether the thesis expressed was right or wrong, whether it was in harmonic accord with history in tune with Darwinism or not (or perhaps not yet)—here at least was a political language with which my imagination could get to grips. And although the phrase was politely applauded by the comrades present, it certainly didn't become the slogan of the day. It was completely submerged by the toasts, the excited editorials and the latest chant from the streets: *Deutsch-land-ein-ig-Vat-er-land.* Shortly afterwards, Oscar Lafontaine was stabbed in the neck by a deranged woman wielding a bread-knife. The world didn't make sense any more.

The full extent of my mental confusion might be made clearer by recounting the following episode from the spring of 1988, when the world was still in order and I felt in touch with events.

I had been invited by an editor on the newspaper *Die Zeit* to contribute to a planned series of articles whose theme was to be 'The Future of German Unity'. I replied by return of post, quite sure of myself, asking him to spare me such nonsense. I had thought about the German question in university history seminars twenty years before, and indeed at that time had spent days and especially nights on end discussing the whole inexhaustible academic subject with my friends. We always came to the same conclusions, namely, that no solution existed to the German question nor was one necessary, since at some point in the future it would dissolve of its own accord in some European soup of the usual sort—at least, that's what we hoped. But since then I had tired of thinking about it. I had no more ideas on the German question. I really couldn't think of a single subject about which I was quite as sick of hearing as the German question, and would he please think of another; God knows there were enough problems on the political agenda, all more important, more urgent and more topical than the completely obsolete question of German unity.

The editor wrote to thank me for my letter and added that he had received similar replies, all turning down the invitation to contribute, from the twenty or thirty other prospective authors, and he had thus decided to drop the idea for the series. That was—I repeat—at the beginning of 1988.

Less than eighteen months later and we were in a fine mess. The pensioner-regime in East Berlin collapsed not with a bang but with a whimper; the previously all-powerful Erich Honecker, who had only recently announced in screeching tones that the Wall would still exist in a hundred years, was robbed overnight of all his offices of state, his apartments, his bank accounts and his porn magazines, and was recovering in a summer-house belonging to a Protestant pastor; a sprightly-looking man by the name of Krenz grinned out at us for a few days from the pages of the newspapers as Head of State of the GDR before disappearing without trace through the stage door, like some figure from a Punch and Judy show who had been hit on the head by a truncheon, only to be replaced by Modrow, the official receiver; a certain Schalck-Golodkowski played a small and obscure role, after which a succession of pale-faced women and bleary-eyed men paraded up and down one after the other—it is impossible to remember all their names—together with bandleaders, writers, lawyers and again and again pastors; all of a sudden the cry at the candle-lit demonstrations changed from 'We are the people' to the already mentioned, curiously idiotic-sounding *'Deutschland-ein-ig-Vat-er-land'*; elections were prescribed, brought forward and held: within a few days a coalition and a democratic government had been formed, within a few weeks it had negotiated and signed a treaty with the Federal Republic, the Deutschmark had been introduced and now, as I write this, even German unity—the very mention of which I, only two years ago, had regarded as political day-dreaming of the most superfluous and superannuated kind—seems to be as good as agreed. No one—at home or abroad—is any longer in any doubt about that, and in another year's time, if not within the next few months, it will be a reality. The speed at which events developed—no, developed is not at all the right expression—the speed at which events burst on to the scene was truly dizzying.

In November 1989, one of the former representatives of the pensioner-regime, the late President of the People's Assembly, Horst Sindermann, spoke the now much quoted words: 'It was as if forty years of socialism had suddenly slid away from under our feet.'

I felt just the same way and so, I suspect, did many of my

contemporaries. Not necessarily forty years of socialism, but forty years of solid European post-war order, rigidly decreed and seemingly unshakeable, slipped right out from under our feet. This was the world we had grown up with. We knew no other.

Not that we held it in great affection, especially its most visible aspects: the division of Europe into East and West, the division of Berlin, the division of the world into two mutually hostile military blocks, each armed to the teeth, seemed to us thoroughly perverse and dangerous—but none the less as a consequence of the world war instigated by Hitler's Germany it was something one had to put up with, and which would only ever change, if at all, over a great number of years, one step at a time. The fact that the tab for the war had to be picked up largely on the other side of the Iron Curtain was regrettable, but unavoidable except at the cost of another war even more devastating than the last.

Of course we were taught at school that the division of Germany was not permanent, that the preamble to the constitution made it the duty of every West German politician to work towards its overthrow, that the Federal Republic and its capital Bonn were simply a provisional arrangement. But we didn't believe that then and we believed it even less with the passing of the years. You don't live for decades in a provisional arrangement—certainly not in one that prospered so magnificently, certainly not when you are young—and when in Sunday speeches the talk was of 'our brothers and sisters in the zone,' or when, just after the building of the Berlin Wall, we were urged to place a lighted advent candle in our windows at night as a sign of national solidarity, it all seemed just as false and ridiculous to us as if someone was seriously asking us to leave our boots in the fireplace so that Santa Claus could fill them with chocolates. No, the unity of the nation—anything at all to do with the nation—didn't interest us one bit. We regarded it as a completely redundant, nineteenth-century idea which had been defeated by history, and one we could happily do without. We couldn't have cared less whether Germany existed as two, three, four or a dozen different states. We went sailing on 17 July. Our relationship with the state in which we lived—the Federal

Republic—was characterized at first by a withdrawn scepticism, later by rebelliousness, then by pragmatism and finally perhaps even by a distanced fondness. This state had proved itself in a far from provisional fashion, it was free, democratic, just and practical—and it was just as old or as young as ourselves, and so, in a certain sense, it was our state.

Otherwise we looked to the west or to the south. Austria, Switzerland, Tuscany, the Veneto, Alsace, Provence, yes, even Crete, Andalusia and the Outer Hebrides—to speak only of Europe—all seemed so much closer than the dubious-sounding statelets of Saxony, Thuringia, Anhalt, Mecklen or Brandenburg, through which we passed, only when it was a necessity, to get on to the transit route to West Berlin. What did we have to do with Leipzig, Dresden or Halle? Nothing. But we had everything to do with Florence, Paris or London. We had hardly heard of towns like Cottbus, Stralsund or Zwickau, a fate which they shared, at least in the eyes of those of us from south of the River Main, with such exotic West German towns as Gütersloh, Wilhelmshaven or Flensburg.

This was our attitude—conscious or unconscious—to the state of the nation, the apparently solid floor that slipped out from under our feet on 9 November. An earthquake, for heaven's sake. With one blow Europe's centre of gravity seemed to have been knocked hundreds of kilometres to the east. Where once there had been a bleak wall that we turned our backs on whenever we could, there had now opened up an unfamiliar, draughty perspective, and we stood around and stared at the new view like cows bewildered at the opening of a long-closed gate, shying away from going through.

It is different for young people, for the twenty- to twenty-five-year-olds, whose historical and political co-ordinates are just beginning to form. For them the end of the cold war, the changes in Eastern Europe and the unification of Germany are the first important political events of their lives and they follow them with a keen interest, if not with enthusiasm. In those hectic November days in Paris I met a young girl who had recently arrived from Berlin to work in France for a few months and learn the language. She was so nervous that she kept sliding off her chair and smoked one cigarette after another—but not because she was abroad alone for the first time and found Paris as interesting and exciting as I had twenty years before. Not a chance. She thought it was 'real stupid' to have to hang around in Paris while 'all the action' was in Berlin. Three days later she could stand it no longer and returned, in order, I assume, to knock bits out of the Wall with her friends, to stroll back and forth across the frontier, to climb around on the Brandenburg gate or breathe the exhaust fumes from the two-stroke cars and to think everything was really great. It reminded me of summer 1968 when we skived off school to go to the anti-Springer demonstration just to get a soaking from the police water-cannon. 'Be where the action is.' Really great!

And the older ones, the mid-fifty- to mid-sixty-year-olds, whose memories stretch back to the pre-partition days and who now sit at the controls of power. For them it is marvellous that once again there is 'movement in European politics'; they beam with confidence and satisfaction at the privilege that has at long last been granted to them: to escape from the shadow of the German political everyday and grab hold of the coat-tails of history with the coming to fruition of the great labour of unification.

And what about the old men? The political and cultural old men of the war and pre-war period, from Stefan Heym to Willy Brandt and even the young-ancient Augstein? They throw themselves into the fray as if they had been doped; as if the German autumn was their last spring, such is the passion with which they engage themselves, make speeches, get involved, moved and incensed, describe events as the fulfilment of their dreams or the beginning of their hopes, write snotty editorials and behave all in all most unlike old men.

We are real old men, the forty-year-old children of the Federal Republic. The earthquake caught us unprepared. It shook us to the marrow. And not just because we had never known an order other than the existing one.

There was another factor: the shock hit us at the worst

conceivable moment, at that age when we tend to take a break, pause, look back, take stock and prepare ourselves bit by bit for the second half of our life, quietly, at a leisurely pace. Nothing is more burdensome in this phase of life than noise and turmoil and the sort of giddy acceleration of events that we are now experiencing, or more to the point, which are now whizzing by over our heads. We thought we had the storms behind us. We imagined we'd come to terms with things, politically as well as in our private lives.

And we thought we had finally succeeded, after so many false starts and twists and turns, in cobbling together a more or less stable picture of the world, like a little chest of drawers with lots of compartments into which we had cleared away and locked up the thousand stumbling blocks of our existence like wooden building bricks, moral and ethical ones in here, political ones here, metaphysical over there, fears and neuroses in here, this way for sex, family, job, money and so on—all carefully packed away, the nursery tidied up at last. (All right, I'll admit it: we took our time about growing up. We were able to take our time, more so than the previous and the succeeding generations; but we made it in the end.)

And just when we thought we had a grip on our lives and had understood the world and thought we knew, at least in broad terms, which way the wind was blowing and which way it would continue to blow—now all of a sudden we are overtaken by a mid-life crisis in the shape of German unity! We could have coped with impotence, with prostate trouble, false teeth, menopause, with a second Chernobyl, with cancer and death and the devil—but not with 'Deutsch-land-ein-ig-Vat-er-land'! That old political chestnut! That oldest of old hat, that we'd long since shoved to the very back of the bottom drawer! Bang—and there it lies, our little chest of drawers, the stumbling blocks strewn all around the room.

'Hold it!' we say, rubbing our eyes in bewilderment, 'Just a moment! What exactly is going on here? And what happens next? German unity? How come? What for? Is that what we actually want?' But before we have even finished asking the question, the answer resounds from all sides—from left and right, from old and young—'The train has left the station.' 'Aha,' we say, not at all prepared for a train journey, 'but is it too late to stop this train? Or at least to steer it in a particular direction? Or perhaps just to brake a little, so that we're not going so fast?'

'Impossible,' say the men of action, the ones who are on top of events. 'It's moving under its own power now. Events are no longer determined by politicians, they determine themselves. One, two, three, history in tune with Darwinism marches rapidly on: monetary union by 1 July—the eastern states are absorbed into the Federal Republic under article 23 of the constitution in the autumn—all-German elections in December—Berlin becomes capital—end of story!'

Berlin as capital, that too! We are to be spared nothing. Is that absolutely necessary, we ask timidly, Berlin as capital? Bonn was quite nice, after all. 'Unrealistic, old man. The train has left the station.'

Fear? No, fear is not the right word. Someone who is suffering from shock feels no fear. I'm still flabbergasted. And I feel a bit queasy, the way you do when you're sitting in a speeding train, travelling over unsafe tracks into unfamiliar surroundings. I have vague misgivings. Not the old ones, that Germany might once again fall into the barbarism and megalomania of the thirties and forties. But rather the worry that all the jealousy and squabbling might lead to serious social tensions at home and, not here, but further east where the Soviet empire is breaking up, to new wars and civil unrest.

Yes, and I'm a bit sad when I think that the rather dull, unloved and pragmatic little state that I grew up in will soon cease to exist.

Translated from the German by Piers Spence

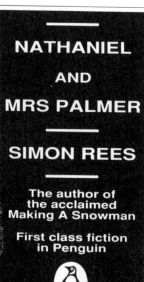

WOLF BIERMANN
FAMILY ARGUMENTS

Christa Wolf has published a story with the title 'What
Remains'*—an unpleasant story from long forgotten
times—and I have been asked to take issue with the
beastly criticisms made by Frank Schirrmacher in the
Frankfurter Allgemeine Zeitung and Ulrich Greiner in *Die Zeit*.
Christa Wolf is accused of cowardice before an enemy, who,
however, was never her enemy and under whose regime the
critics never had to live. Tricky!

The critics accuse Christa Wolf of only now pulling out of
the drawer an anti-Stasi story that she wrote more than ten years
ago—now, that is, when it won't cost her anything to publish it.
True! True, even though it was only yesterday that the author
was a holy cow. Why do these knights of the intellect only now
assault the flattered author, when it likewise doesn't cost them
anything to do so? However hesitant, timid and torn Christa
Wolf was, she never played the hero, and that's why she was
allowed to be torn, timid and hesitant. Apart from that one

---

*Christa Wolf's 'What Remains', first published in English
in *Granta* 33, describes the experience of being watched and
followed by Stasi agents. In Germany, the piece has been at the
centre of an extraordinary controversy that was engendered by
two powerful attacks, one by the critic Frank Schirrmacher and
the other by Ulrich Greiner. Schirrmacher, calling Wolf an
opportunist and an apologist for totalitarianism, dismisses her
article, which he says was written in 1979 and rewritten ten years
later after the collapse of the Honecker regime. It is, according
to Schirrmacher, 'sentimental and unbelievable to the point of
kitsch'. Greiner accuses Wolf of being a dupe and a coward, and
also asks why it took so long for the article to be published: had
it appeared at the time, it would have been heroic; now it is
simply pathetic.

Wolf Biermann was born in Hamburg at the start of the war
and emigrated to East Germany in 1953. In 1965 he was banned
from publishing or performing in public, and, in 1976, after
being granted permission to give a concert in West Germany, he
was not allowed to return to East Berlin.

should judge the apple tree by its fruits and not by whether it's good for making cudgels or firewood for a burning at the stake.

The cowardlybrave intellectuals of the GDR are certainly in a corner. Not only Christa Wolf, but also such shrunken dragon-slayers as my false friend Stefan Heym, my false foe Stephan Hermlin, or Volker Braun whose talent I admire, or Fritz Cremer whom I feel sorry for, or Scheumann whom I don't know, or Hermann Kant whom I fear and Peter Hacks whom I despise, Rainer Kirsch whom I couldn't care less about, Erik Neutsch who will always remain dim, and Willi Sitte who also once wanted to do something better for himself and the world.

I know a few of these selfless pensioners of Stalinism: half-hearted mutineers, who are now shaken by worries about how to survive. Nothing but sufferings of luxury. Party poets who now numbly learn that the villa is Western property. State artists, who must look on as their state disappears. Sticklers for the truth with all their crocheted self-deceptions. Kickers against the pricks with blocked pension rights. Preachers of equality with threatened privileges. Underground fighters without lucrative state commissions. Free spirits, troublesomely burdened with national prizes.

Now they're all being given a moral MOT by Western critics. All these ramshackle Eastern cars are being driven over the pit and some smart engineer from the review pages is poking a screwdriver through all the rusty holes in the floor without the least bit of piety. Oh, and the moral exhaust test! The oil with which it was greased and coated is burning up. In the East there's the stink of self-pity.

And so the question: can such flippant, cheeky, snot-nosed children like Frank Schirrmacher of the *Frankfurter Allgemeine Zeitung* and Ulrich Greiner of *Die Zeit*, who never went through what we suffered during the Stalin period, be allowed to pass judgement? Stupid question, stupid answer: yes of course they can, and they should too.

It's not easy talking to all the old leftists in the West now; they are unpleasantly confused, if not disappointed, and even irritated that the GDR live-animal experiment has ended. They resent that those from the GDR failed to build the socialism that those in the West had always dreamed possible—even though there are many on the left here who, although they don't admit it, are in fact extremely relieved that their ideal remained a dream, and that it is one they never had to live.

And in the East? The writers and painters already long sustained by their earnings here, or the actors and theatre directors on loan, seen from time to time grazing in the West, or the musicians on hire, accustomed to poaching in the West now all sneer at the banana-hungry excitement of the GDR rabble at the bargain counters of the West German department stores. These are East-West figures and they, too, would have happily borne the Eastern live-animal experiment for another thousand years. Some are actually annoyed that the Wall has fallen. In the last few years many had got their foreign travel passports—the imprisoned populace bitterly called them Aryan passes. And they paid enviably low taxes on their Western royalties—fifteen per cent. There are those for whom a human right tastes twice as sweet, if it can also be enjoyed as a privilege.

Brecht in his *Tui* novel fragment distinguishes the genuine intellectuals from the 'Tellectuelinns' whom he coldly abbreviates as *Tuis*. *Tuis* are the bought intellectuals, hired to produce ideology. They are the brain athletes, who hire out their head just as the workers do their hands. A vivid picture of transferred identities. But we are not on the stage of the Berlin Brecht Museum among the congress of washerwomen: in reality there is no either-or, but a not-only-but-also. We are all both free and chained and are always muddling up one with the other. No apostle of truth gets by without self-deceptions.

And so on the occasion of these upheavals we once more have to think about the ancient questions: what should the writer do in the dark times of tyranny?

Go too far, certainly. But how far too far?

Deal out truths, for god's sake, yes! But when and how and how many and to whom?

Be truthful by all means! But what is to be done, if one's life is at stake and not just the good life?

Appeals? But why tear open the shirt of someone without a heart!

Judgements? Why stop the mouth of a dead man!
Be afraid, who would not be? But what if fear has me?
Justice is a dream, old as oppression. I too dream of a politics which is moral. And who wouldn't desire a morality which at last becomes practical politics? We all dream of paradise; it is the conventional dream in hell.

In the East the devil's instruments were power, privileges, connections. Today the same things are regulated by money. So the New Testament was stronger than the Communist Manifesto. Do you remember George Orwell's apt aphorism? 'Faith, love, hope, these three; but the greatest of these is money.'

Money is now the common theme in the GDR. The workers have begun to do their sums; the farmers have drawn up balance sheets; the more clever functionaries practise capitalism without sentimentality. It's only the few intellectuals, artists, writers who shed tears for the familiar misery and give it nicknames like: the GDR identity; what was worth preserving; the unique cultural values. When we look more closely we can calmly say money here too.

On the night after *the* football game I turned from television to the streets. I walked through West Berlin and then over to the East. I wanted to make a comparison. The West made me want to vomit; the East scared me. On the Kurfürstendamm, the fans were roaring: *Olé Olé Olé!* And then: *Sieg! Sieg! Sieg!* But the windows of the expensive shops were not broken. There were only flags held from car windows, horns blaring and empty beer cans strewn about like the cartridges of discharged shells. Oh, what a lovely football war!

Then in the East, I reached Alexanderplatz. Shaven half-children were chasing Vietnamese, who ran panting towards me and my wife and then fled round the old city hall behind the builders' huts. In Rosa Luxemburg Strasse there were figures, staggering in their drunkenness, smashing the display windows with bars. They thrust their arms into the air for Heil Hitler and grabbed an old man—'Reply with the German greeting!'—but he

was slow responding and they beat him to the ground. They
roared:

And today Germany belongs to us
And tomorrow the whole wide world . . .

Always these two lines from the old Nazi song. Where do
they know them from? We ducked away to the side. The shaven
half-children moved off, stumbling up Schönhauser Allee towards
Prenzlauer Berg for the traditional street fight with the punks. In
the East the punks are recruited principally from the children of
the intellectual semi-opposition. They have a diffuse leftism and
despise the compromises of their rebellious parents. My wife
pulled me away. She was afraid that these boozed-up friends of
football would knock my mouth to the back of my head, only
because they had got me mixed up with Wolf Biermann, but she
had to shout at me before I would leave: I couldn't see enough of
these Goya ghosts. These half-children, our 'skins', are drawn
from everywhere, but most are the children of functionaries,
police and Stasi men, who, out of a job, now brood at home in
front of the television, drinking. There's continuity amid the
upheaval: the children of the opposition of yesterday beat up the
children of the establishment. The sleep of reason breeds
monsters.

The Cold War is over, and this is what the peace celebrations
look like. Well, good, Communism has capitulated. But who has
actually lost? Erich Honecker? He grins in bewilderment and
pisses himself into the grave. The henchman Wolfgang Biermann,
the feared managing director of Zeiss-Jena? My namesake went
to the West long ago and is now speculating with the pound,
applying his expert knowledge in the accelerating trade with the
East. The directors of the state enterprises? Many long ago set up
companies under civil law and plucked the best bits out of the
bankrupt's assets for peanuts. The people? The assembly line
workers? The farmers in the collectives? Nonsense! They never
got, and never believed in, anything. One can only lose illusions
that one actually has.

The losers are a handful of left-wing intellectuals. In the
name of genuine Marxism and true Socialism we had become

locked into the dispute with the Party. But our opponents have been out of reach for a long time. And we, a small band of the more or less upright, crouch at the grave and chew at the corpse of Communism. We know too much, which is why we are the biggest suckers of all. Our memory is too sharp, which is why, as the new market economy takes off, we stand apathetically on the side watching it leave.

Among us, there are some who risked and suffered more than others, and we therefore accused each other because of it. But from the great vantage place of history, these are trifling differences. In the end it's very simple: we have all come out of the same historical hope.

We did not, after all, set out, like the Fascists, to place one nation above all others and to exterminate whole peoples. Communism was part of the humanist tradition of the Enlightenment, before it became the mass grave of the Enlighteners. We wanted a life before death and wanted to bring the Jewish-Christian paradise down to earth. Our ancestors are the radical democratic Jacobins, the Icarian dreamers, the slaughtered Communards in Paris, the sailors who were gunned down in Kronstadt and in the royal mews in Berlin in December 1918. People of our sort live and work in the kibbutzim—the only example of a halfway successful socialism.

During the difficult years when I was still living in East Germany and my work was banned, I sang in Chausseestrasse, in East Berlin, about our torn Germany:

I lie in the better half
And feel a double pain . . .

The right was offended by the provocative words 'better half' and still throws them in my face today. The left, however, finds fault with the little word 'pain' and gets into a rage because this pain was a double pain! That's how to fall between stools.

For whole nights on end we talked till our mouths were dry. Again and again such cowardlybrave friends of freedom as Heym, Hermlin and Christa Wolf accused me (and others) of going too far.

Sometimes the dispute between us became so paramount that we forgot that the cretins in the Politbureau were in fact our real (and very deadly) enemies. But everything was awkwardly mixed up. At that time Christa Wolf was a candidate for the Central Committee; she supported the invasion of Czechoslovakia. Hermlin had in the hated and feared Erich Honecker a loyal friend from his youth, whom he could call at any time and ask for help. Similarly, the world famous Heiner Müller: his friend was Manfred Wekwerth, also Honecker's confidant. A few people could be helped.

And despite everything, we are aware that there is a yes and a no, and that, again and again, there is a right and a wrong. But never a simple right or a simple wrong. How far is too far? There were ideological acrobats who, with their feet in both camps, constantly jumped from one to the other. We had deep family relations with our deadly enemies and we never broke them. I was no different. At least I wasn't any different until the notorious Eleventh Plenum in November 1965, when I was finally and completely banned. The verdict was my good fortune, because I would have ended up compromised as well.

Before that I had even occasionally met Margot Honecker. I visited her in her ministry near the Brandenburg Gate. She made an effort and kept on at me. I was young, and she wanted to save me. She even had herself driven to 131 Chausseestrasse in her state limousine, swayed in mink up the two flights of stairs and paid a surprise visit on me in my hovel. 'Wolf,' she said, 'see reason. No more songs like these! You're going too far! If you would only see reason—you could be our best poet . . .' Yes, it's a joke: the uneducated old maid was handing out certificates for the best poets of the GDR! But that's how intoxicated with themselves they were. And that's how we talked to one another: yes, we were enemies, enemies to the last breath; but we were family.

I carried the family argument further than Christa Wolf. I happened to have the black good luck of my father dying in Auschwitz and not in Stalingrad. My childhood was not just different; I had nothing to atone for. And I had nothing to prove to the new rulers. I spoke with the arrogant voice of the legitimate political heir. And that was also why I didn't speak in servile language in my songs. I loved more childishly and hated more childishly and despised more wildly and . . . I respected those old comrades more than the children of the Nazis ever could. Their wretched modesty didn't fit with my biography. I fought naïvely and without guard, and I always spoke plainly, even in rhyme. The consequences were inevitable.

They were detestable times and, despite everything, interesting ones. But isn't it a comfort! At last we have new problems. Let there be new disputes too, please!

After this glut of historic days, I at last hurled myself into the North Sea again for a swim. Having to spend so much time turning with each new wind, one hardly has time for such trifles as a swim in the North Sea. A ban on swimming was announced that day—spur enough for me. A westerly gale threw up large and powerful waves, but I wasn't going to be deterred. I didn't, however, manage to get past the breakers. The waves picked up my 150 pounds and hurled it against the sand. And then masses of ebbing water dragged me by force away from the beach and pulled me under water, thrusting me dangerously against the breakwater. I was afraid and aware of myself.

That's how afraid people in the GDR are now about rents and wages and about the price of milk. And that's how afraid Christa Wolf may now feel, caught by the waves of the press. Oh the foaming of the press! The productivity of industrial societies is devastating. You can purchase any number of printing presses and any quantity of paper. You can start newspapers and magazines and then find the people to buy them. There are difficulties, though, in expanding the production of intellectual matter that has to go inside.

It was terrible during Stalinism. A critical remark in a *Pravda* article and a writer's life was destroyed. When I landed in the West, I read every review with great attention. And when some idiot wanted to make a name for himself at my expense, then I hysterically imagined that higher powers, my well-organized enemies, had set him on me. Only slowly did I grasp

241

the banal truth. Here in the West every dunderhead is allowed to do what he wants, as long as it sells, which is why, perhaps, one is best off with established journalists in established newspapers: only someone who has already made it in the market-place can, ignoring the market-place, occasionally afford an opinion and speak about matters he understands. Frank Schirrmacher and Ulrich Greiner are in this category; they have started an overdue debate.

In any case, more important than what is written about us is what we write. We, with our longer breath, will have the last laugh.

When this Greater German muddle is over, it's only our novels, plays, poems and songs that will count. That is comfort and stimulus enough for me. I'm looking forward to the next story from Christa Wolf and I'm eager to find out if Heiner Müller will discover a meaning in history after all. I'm certain that Günter Kunert will continue to deliver what Marcel Reich-Ranicki calls 'good product'. And Jürgen Fuchs, whom I admire so much, will still write prose, that fills our stomachs like the good dry bread of justice. Of course, I see black—that is, black-red-gold—but I'm still happy that the damned tyranny has crumbled. The party's over; much hope has been downed like cheap booze. The result is a heavy head. And so now I sing against the left hangover:

> *Who preaches hope, well, he's lying. Yet who*
> *Kills hope, is a worthless hound*
> *And I do both and cry: Please*
> *Take, all that you need!*
> *(too much is dangerous) . . .*

Oh, and the utopias. Only who changes remains true to himself! They rise into the sky and shine and turn pale and then just disappear. So what? The longing of mankind for a juster society is born anew with each generation. We cannot do otherwise and neither do we want to.

Translated from the German by Martin Chalmers

ALLAN GURGANUS
THE RAMADA
INN AT SHILOH

A ll I really know about my great-grandfathers is that they tried to kill each other at the Battle of Shiloh. Opponents, one Southern, one not. The Carolina Regular was sixteen; the Volunteer from Ohio had just gone eighteen. Both hailed from semi-prosperous farms; both possessed tenor voices considered notable in parlours back home; both were the eldest of eight. Of course, they did not know each other. Not until much later when they met, united states, in me.

According to their letters, each boy spent three war years scared half witless. Each admitted that fear makes a fellow's fingertips go numb. Each expressed an early terror of battle's sound. Those deafening sophisticated munitions predicted our century. Imagine you are a country kid and the loudest noise you know is one bronze church bell in the nearby village or your squirrel gun or your hound's barking. A commotion? All three sounds at once. Compare this to cannonades that shook, then levelled, Tennessee's ancient oaks, or to the volleys that caused mules to lift then lower their long ears and, eyes pressed shut, evacuate. Noise of this force finds your sternum first, plucks your rib-cage like some harp of tin. We all know such blasts from discos, jets, the jeremiads of haywire car alarms. The world's pulse is now a nerve-ripping roar. We hardly notice. They did. 'Dear Momma,' my Southern kinsman wrote,

> the sound of cannons and all is the worst of it so far. You first hear it from some considerable miles away. That will surely put the person on his guard way far in advance of there being one thing you can really do about it. No sound we ever heard touches a battle's for loudness, as it is more like thunder but close down to the earth and man-made. You cannot tell which side causes which part of the sound. I shall simply call it 'fearful' and, in ending, endeavour to ask that you pass along my love to Emily et al.

I have their letters, cross-written to save paper. I live with daguerreotypes that show me my own features, pickled, sub-contracted. The Northerner would recall Shiloh as the meadow where his leg got shot clear through; I am told that forever after he walked with a dreadful wobble, couldn't cross the room without a cane. As a kid in North Carolina, I believed my Southern great-grandad had crippled my Yankee one. Though statistically unlikely, couldn't it have happened?

L ast month, having imagined such a quest since I was five, confessing the reason only to my brilliant travel agent, I took a few days off work and rented a very red semi-sportscar and—one hour after deciding— drove south towards Shiloh. The luxury was explaining it to no one. Bachelors are lucky. The agent booked me a room 'with instant off-ramp battlefield access', a term she read aloud from her computer screen. I propped my kinsmen's images on the rented crimson dashboard, plastic-leather. 'Men after death,' Nietzsche advises, 'are understood worse than men of the moment, but *heard* better.'

The original Shilo was a Canaanite town that became sanctuary for the Israelite confederacy (twelfth-eleventh century BC). There the Ark of the Covenant was installed till the Philistines captured it. Soon after, Shilo was destroyed (around 1050 BC). My great-grandads' Shiloh (also known as the Battle of Pittsburg Landing) proved the second great engagement of the Civil War. It cost each side 10,000 to 12,000 casualties a day, meaning 6 and 7 April, 1862 AD.

While driving, I listen to country music and sing hymns aloud. The radio gives bulletins about the Middle East, and I begin recalling certain jellying fears not felt since 1966, my endless bus ride to Great Lakes Naval Training Center. This was basic training for my own four-year role in another war (Vietnam). I'm feeling certain panicked draftee sensations well-suppressed for twenty years. There exists one awful pre-Southeast Asia studio photo portrait of me, shaved bald under my sailor hat, black bags cut beneath the eyes by boot-camp double pneumonia; I am pale with my struggle to look cocky. I see someone imitating a guy who can plan his fate! 'The first qualification for a historian,' Stendhal writes, 'is to have no ability to invent.' My forefathers and myself, we pass muster.

Closing in on Shiloh, I understand: my geeky portrait looks

like these young chumps on my dashboard. Only semi-handsome in tintypes intended as family keepsakes just in case. Slow film emulsion required a nineteenth-century sitter really to sit, one to three minutes, eyes unblinking, a hidden clamp biting the uppermost vertebrae. You adopted not some transient smile notoriously hard to maintain, but the very dour and therefore practicable face you'd wear into Eternity.

On the way to their battlefield, I reduce my own coerced military career (1966–70 AD), meaning my entire eighteenth and nineteenth and twentieth and twenty-first years, to a single word: humiliation.

And driving, I decide things. I do this with the untested grandeur peculiar to solitary trips across great distances in new red vehicles operated with gleeful if unnoted male skill. Heart crossed by seat-belt, I recall my single favourite testament of the Civil War: the nurse Walt Whitman's quickly jotted hospital journals, our literature's rarest distillation of all wars' pathos, all wars' waste:

> Wm. Von Vliet, Co. #. 89th New York. Bed 37.—shell wound in the arm—Gave 20 cts.—Wants some smoking tobacco & pipe—arm amp.—turn out bad—died poor boy.

> Hiram Scholis—bed 3—Ward E.—26th N. York— wants some pickles—a bottle of pickles.

I allow myself to stop at a Dunkin' Donuts. I buy one horrifically sweet thing so filled with gory cherry-dyed jam, it reminds me of the war I plan to visit and so, after a single gruesome bite, I spare myself the calories. Out the open window it sails. Middle age is, paradoxically, the great moment for such impulsive deeds and treks. Because: (a) you can finally afford the car, the motel room, the time; (b) there's all that accrued inertia to create the contrast, ballast.

I tell the car: I think Lincoln's face predicted the twentieth century.

How else does our insomnia find so much of itself creased there in that witty grieving gaze? It seems to anticipate its own assassination; it is less concerned with that, far more worried for us. Lincoln's face is beaten to the surface, a private pocket worn inside out. Its humanity and shrewd wasted wisdom almost shame and terrify us now. (Lincoln was once called two-faced by a lady journalist. He laughed a rusted stove-pipe laugh we all can imagine if we try. Lincoln said, 'If I were two-faced, Madam, would I be wearing THIS one?')

I long for leaders who can tell us stories all their own. I long for personal content not ceded to young Ivy speech writers. I'd love someone Lincoln-like who thinks in narrative beginnings, middles, ends; someone who has held at least one job previous to being Rich then Veep then Chief Exec. Our contemporary leaders' features are praised as 'boyishly handsome'. This means untouched by experience. We seem to value that. This fear of maturity might be the gauge of our contradiction as a people: middle-aged yet endlessly adolescent. Lincoln, self-taught and self-made, looks hand-carved the hard way. He has been torn by the climb into authority, by odd jobs and the wearing widening gyre of his epic human understanding for all persons, of all races and—we know now—all times. He is a man vast as the conflict he navigated.

Consider our recent actor of a President. One study found that during his eighth and last year in office, his most oft-repeated sentences were 'Nobody told me' and 'I don't remember'. Chuckling, he left mere telling and remembering (any leader's holiest function) to unworthy others. And, how popular he was! Friends, if memory serves, I think we have lost something. We have become a nation of amnesiacs, frequent flyers bent on endlessly upgrading to first class. Lincoln remembers. And therefore is remembered: Picasso owned a large collection of Lincolnalia and told Gertrude Stein that Lincoln was 'le Quixote USA'. Marilyn Monroe pronounced Lincoln 'the sexiest man in American history' and claimed she married Arthur Miller because of his Lincolnly length and raw-boned face. To quote a recent novel: 'Lincoln's smile is like a muddy country crossroad that—when rain has stopped—dries to show you every single wagon, bird and walker that has ever passed across it.'

I wonder: why does the plight of my dashboard's child-crusaders suddenly feel so familiar? Why should they seem closer

to my heart than their contemporary equivalents: young GIs off
to Saudi Arabia for 'Operation Desert Shield'. You see them each
night on American television, 'public service TV spots'. A square-
face sunburned boy grins, against an eternity of sand:

> My name's Corporal Clayton Plante from Falls, North
> Carolina. Hi, Mom. I'm eating okay, so don't worry.
> Just keep that '64 T-bird's battery cranked up. And,
> ahem, Tiffany? Honey, just know I love you ver', ver'
> much.

Why is it easier to empathize with the missing farmboys
from a missing bucolic country? Their girl-friends would have
been called Prudence or Chastity or Hope—named by their rural
parents who valued the qualities of prudence and chastity and
hope. Nobody then would have been named in honour of a
Manhattan jewellery store, by parents who thought 'Tiffany'
sounded classy and do not know why. Tiffany is the tenth most
popular girl's name in the United State today. Our hearts are ads
for stores we cannot afford yet. So, yes, Lincoln, we miss. And
also the loyal, plain and pure Emily. MIA.

South-west Tennessee. Here already. The sign insists, 'Shiloh
Battlefield Closes At Sunset.' Like so many official
statements, this proves something of a lie. Into opposite
jacket pockets I slip my oxidized daguerreotypes. Armed with
maps and no sense of direction, I still manage to pace off the
crucial sweeps. I factor for the presence of a thousand horses and
for a mat of human forms you could walk across without once
touching meadow's soil. Imagining the sound, I have ancestral
stage directions: 'Like thunder but closer to the earth and man-
made. You cannot tell which part of it is from which side.' How
quiet out here, meadowlarks minimum. I stride along General
Johnston's route; to one side, there is a wood where both side's
untested troops fired face-to-face at point-blank range. I find the
very spot (I think, then know) where my Yankee forbear
sacrificed his leg. I sit precisely there.

Beyond hardwood trees, the Tennessee River makes sweet
steady surgings. Flowering with sneezy tassled weeds, the

Allan Gurganus

meadow around me looks inevitable—as I'd imagined it—better, prettier, but more forgetful. All I know about my great-grandfathers is that they tried to kill each other here. Strangers to one another, as to me, they were eldest sons, as I'm the eldest of four sons. They were both musical and, like me, their families' joker-peacemaker and birthday-rememberer. From mildly respectable Protestant farms: seven hundred acres of North Carolina, three hundred of Ohio. So alike, these enemies I never met outside daguerreotypes and rumour. And so like me. They were told what to do, and they did it and they paid with legs and with decades of the nightmares.

The famous pathos of battlefields rests in just how readily green forgives everything. How fast an Evil Empire is overtaken by goodly growth! This vista—so still and rolling—resembles its fine and somehow manly name, 'Shiloh'.

I settle in the high grass where one ancestor lost something. I feel, slumped here, a strange exhaustion so profound it registers as an almost erotic stirring. Calming bird-calls, fast clean clouds. The day is ending over me too soon. At Shiloh, dusk's blood-reds mean more, its vaulting blues and greys are tonight equally represented. I stretch out here fearful that the park ranger, seeing my red car alone in the lot, will come stalking me, like my boy-forbears, an interloper half-apologetic at even being here.

I lean back, hands laced behind my head, tweed coat inappropriate, but what uniform would be right? As everything darkens, I am mostly listening. First, to the crickets taking up their sing-song signalling. I can hear moving vans lumbering along the highway not far off (unemployed Northerners seeking work here in the still-prospering South, the losing side). Night-hawks and killdeers cry. The grass is getting damp and so am I, sleeves, the upturned collar, my pockets knocking as with castanets, genetic platelets, these tintypes of boy-targets. I wait in this lush forgiving meadow, but for what? To hear something maybe?

I consider the motel suite, guaranteed by credit card, waiting for whatever use I care to make of its attendant pleasures, room service, club sandwiches, champagne, the cable channel's soft-core porn, the jacuzzi, the fax machine. But, by accident, winded after the long drive, jumpy with a caffeinated tourist excitement,

250

all concentration shot, gratitude becoming exhaustion, I fall to sleep out here in the weeds at Shiloh. Ill-equipped and right in the open, the way, I figure, they slept.

At three a.m., I wake. Where am I? Then I know I'm doing what those boys did. Scared kids, eyes opening, half-sitting with a lurch. Boys touching their damp tunics, they fear the worst—Shot? Hurt yet? No? Good—and still in America yet feeling so far from their younger sisters, their parents' fertile farms. I prop myself on either elbow. Nobody knows where I am, nobody but this family battlefield.

I listen. Men after death are *heard* better. The crickets have given up; the truck traffic seems thinner. What I catch is what anybody hears in the middle of a field preparing itself for dawn: the slight hiss of uplifting condensation and the old invisibles of a place alive in the dark. A rabbit or something thumps directly past by me, unalarmed—scaring me but good. And in the silence afterward, I tell you what I hear. It is not quite a sound, not quite a smell or a sensed humidity. If it is about to be sound, it still rests curled on the far side of actual hearing. But as darkness deepens just before first light, something else comes cresting—part sense, part fear, part disorientation and backache, part superstition. I know. There is a breathing consciousness out here. It is not quite sad. Its neutrality proves its presence to me. Here I am, damp and urban and comical and on my back under the same stars that knew this field on 6 and 7 April, 1862, AD—when men I am like and unlike rested here doing just this, face-up, thinking of absent beloved chaste girls, secret spots in farm outbuildings, and not of any foolish future kinsman who might come and try to meet them finally. I can tell you that it hangs just at tree-top level all around this meadow's edge. It is a whisper that makes me, here in the weeds, perk like some rabbit on the first dawn of hunting season. And the collective electric field out here, pooled—the hurt and dead and those who escaped with only the memory, they all ask—if I may reduce the curled hunch into three mere words of English.

First 'Why me?'

And then 'Why?'

L imping to the one car in the parking lot, also drenched with Shiloh's lavish somehow-gory dew, having been computer-billed for a room I haven't seen, I find that my jacket smells of woodsmoke. Is that still embedded in the bled-on dirt, my recent bed? And how good it is to ache this way this morning and, for once, to know why. To have come here and found something. But what? That Shiloh Battlefield does not close at sunset: it has been open twenty-four hours a day since that April of cannon fire and dreadful human cries.

In the de-idealized age of Quayle and Bush, Lee, Lincoln, Douglass and Whitman appear to belong not just to another time and race but another species. That early war proved that the most fearful rivalries are family ones, that no poison from without can match those liquid hexes we have brewed as by-products of our luck. We gaze back to a time when every general was awarded some fond nickname by his troops. Our current leaders with their tax-sheltered faces would simply stand there, born to privilege, devoid of any true occupation's lore or usefulness, 'boyishly handsome' unto senility, as they watched the astounding General John Hood, apostle-handsome in his beard, already missing limbs he'd sacrificed in earlier exploits, literally tie himself with ropes on to his horse for the day's battle.

O Captain! my Captain! our fearful trip is done,
The ship has weather'd every rack, the prize we sought is
won,
The port is near, the bells I hear, the people all exulting,
While follow eyes the steady keep, the vessel grim and
daring;
    But O heart! heart! heart!
      O the bleeding drops of red,
        Where on the deck my Captain lies,
        Fallen cold and dead.

My Captain does not answer, his lips are pale and still,
My father does not feel my arm, he has no pulse nor will,
The ship is anchor'd safe and sound, its voyage closed and
done,
From fearful trip the victor ship comes in with object won;

Exult O shores, and ring O bells!
But I with mournful tread,
Walk the deck my Captain lies,
Fallen cold and dead.

At peace, do we feel besieged? Still fairly prosperous, don't we feel poor. Governed, we feel robbed. Lonely, we're a crowd. We all have "instant offramp battlefield access". We are at war again and we do not know why. And who decides?

The motel room nearby has already been computer-charged to my account whether or not I stay there. But I won't be needing it. I'm still out in here the middle of a field. Face up and fearful of dawn's cannons, somehow aimed at us—by us. And we feel chilled out here and my bed is mostly rocks, and we keep wondering: if we are alive right here on my own native soil then, beloved fellow citizen of our great saved republic, why, oh why, do we still feel so far from home?

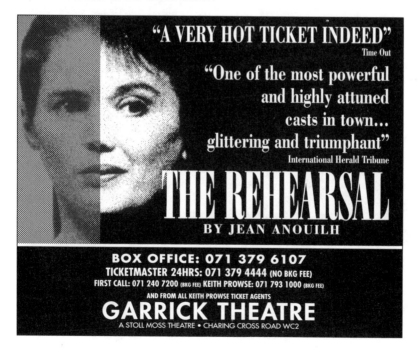

Notes on Contributors

John le Carré's most recent book is *The Secret Pilgrim*, published in January. A film based on one of his early books, *A Murder of Quality*, will shortly appear on Thames Television. **Alex Kayser** is a Swiss-born portrait photographer. He has been photographing bankers since commissioned by *Fortune* eight years ago. **Max Frisch** published his first book in 1940. 'Switzerland Without an Army?' was first published in German as a pamphlet around the time of the Swiss referendum to abolish the military. The referendum was defeated by a vote of 1,903,797 (64.4 per cent) to 1,052,218 (35.6 per cent). **Friedrich Dürrenmatt**'s address to Václav Havel is adapted from the speech he delivered on awarding the Gottlieb Duttweiler Prize to the Czechoslovak President on 22 November 1990. Dürrenmatt died on 14 December 1990. **John Berger**'s novel *Lilac and Flag* completes his trilogy *Into their Labours*. It has been published by Granta Books along with the paperback of *Once in Europa*, the second volume of the trilogy, a collection of love stories. **Jean Mohr** has collaborated with John Berger on three books, *A Fortunate Man*, *Another Way of Telling* and *A Seventh Man*. He lives in Geneva. 'In Summer Camps' is the first two chapters of a work-in-progress by **Jayne Anne Phillips**. Her previous stories in *Granta* include 'Rayme—a Memoir of the Seventies' (*Granta* 8) and 'Fast Lanes' (*Granta* 19). **Nadine Gordimer**'s last novel, *My Son's Story*, was published last year. She lives in Johannesburg. **Patrick Süskind** is the author of three novels, *Perfume*, *The Double Bass* and *The Pigeon*. 'A Battle' was published in *Granta* 21, 'The Story-teller'. **Wolf Biermann** is a poet, singer and playwright, as known for his music and cabaret performances as his writings. **Allan Gurganus**'s novella 'Blessed Assurance' was published in *Granta* 32, 'History'. A collection of his stories, *White People*, will be published by Faber & Faber and Alfred A. Knopf later this year.

Alex Kayser's bankers, on pages 78 and 79, are Robert Holzach (Union Bank of Switzerland), Nikolaus Senn (Union Bank of Switzerland), Alfred Sarasin (A. Sarasin & CIE), Thierry Barbey (Lombard Odier & CIE), Rainer Gut (Credit Suisse), Roberts Jeker (Credit Suisse), Hans Vontobel (J. Vontobel & CIE), Hans Joerg Vontobel (J. Vontobel & CIE), Nicolas Baer (Bank Julius Baer), Hans Bar (Bank Julius Bar), Peter Baer (Bank Julius Baer), Franz Lutolf (Swiss Bank Corporation).